Use of Public-Private Partnerships to Meet Future Army Needs

Ike Y. Chang
Steven Galing
Carolyn Wong
Howell Yee
Elliot I. Axelband
Mark Onesi
Kenneth P. Horn

Prepared for the
United States Army

Arroyo Center

RAND

Approved for public release; distribution unlimited

For more information on the RAND Arroyo Center, contact the Director of Operations, (310) 393-0411, extension 6500, or visit the Arroyo Center's Web site at http://www.rand.org/organization/ard/

PREFACE

This report documents the principal findings of a study on exploring innovative ways for acquiring advanced technologies to meet future Army needs—namely, using public-private partnerships (PPPs). This report is an updated and expanded version of a paper presented at the Army Materiel Command (AMC) Executive Steering Committee meeting in April 1997. At that time, the focus of the study was limited to generating revenue from research and development (R&D) opportunities and infrastructure assets. The research was broadened to examine other advantages of PPPs. This report examines the overall utility of PPPs from the Army's perspective.

The research was sponsored by Mr. Michael Fisette, Principal Deputy for Technology, HQ AMC, and was conducted within the Force Development and Technology Program of the RAND Arroyo Center. The Arroyo Center is a federally funded research and development center sponsored by the United States Army.

The findings should be of interest to Army audiences addressing strategies for developing advanced technology as well as those concerned with infrastructure assets and installation closures. This research was completed and approved for public release in 1998.

UA
25
.5
.U83
1999

CONTENTS

Preface	iii
Figures	ix
Tables	xi
Summary	xiii
Acknowledgments	xxi
Acronyms	xxiii

Chapter One
   INTRODUCTION 1
   Definition of Public-Private Partnership 2
   Benefits of Public-Private Partnerships 2
      Leverage Assets, Reduce Costs, or Decrease Outlays ... 3
      Increase Value of Army Assets 4
      Create New Army Capabilities and Assets 4
      Early Influence on Technology 5
      Improve Readiness Posture 5
      Generate Revenue 6
   Objective and Scope 6
   Background 7
   Organization 10

Chapter Two
   THE COMPLEMENTARY CONTRIBUTIONS IN
   PUBLIC-PRIVATE PARTNERSHIPS 11
   Army Contributions 11
   Private-Sector Contributions 11

Marketing Expertise	12
Access to Capital	14
Access to Leading-Edge Technology	15
Operating Expertise	16

Chapter Three
THE TREND TOWARD INCREASED USE OF
PUBLIC-PRIVATE PARTNERSHIPS 19
Legislative Changes	19
Stevenson-Wydler Technology Innovation Act of 1980	20
Grants	20
Technology Transfer Act of 1986	21
Cooperative Agreements	22
Other Transactions	22
Other Transactions for Prototyping	23
Test and Evaluation	24
National Technology Transfer and Advancement Act of 1995 (NTTAA)	25
Proposed Technology Transfer Commercialization Act of 1997 (TTCA)	25
Leases on Non-Excess Property	26
Actions by Organizations Within the Department of Defense	27
Quadrennial Defense Review	27
National Defense Panel	28
Plan for Consolidation of Defense Labs and T&E Centers	29
Defense Science Board Studies	29
Actions By Specific Commands and Agencies	30
Activities at the Local Government Level	30
Setting the Trend	32
Infrastructure PPPs	32
Intellectual Property PPPs	34
Financial Arrangement PPPs	35

Chapter Four
A PROJECTED EVALUATION OF PUBLIC-PRIVATE
PARTNERSHIPS 39
Feasibility Criteria	41
Legality	41
Acceptance	43

Attractiveness to Private Firms	43
Evaluation of Specific Ideas	44
Infrastructure	44
Intellectual Property	46
Financial Arrangements	50

Chapter Five
    CLOSING REMARKS AND RECOMMENDATIONS 55

Appendix

A.	SUMMARIES OF SPECIFIC IDEAS	59
B.	LIST OF EXAMPLES	73

Bibliography 83

FIGURES

1.1. Army Research Budget for Fiscal Years 1984–2003 . . .   8
3.1. Timeline of Major Legislative Actions Affecting PPPs . 21
4.1. Screening Tool for Identifying Promising Candidates . 40

TABLES

S.1.	Evaluation Criteria	xviii
3.1.	Estimated Revenues Generated from Army PPPs in FY95	33
4.1.	Feasibility of PPP Ideas in Infrastructure	45
4.2.	Potential Benefits of PPP Ideas for Infrastructure	47
4.3.	Feasibility of PPP Ideas in Intellectual Property	48
4.4.	Potential Benefits of PPP Ideas for Intellectual Property	49
4.5.	Feasibility of PPP Ideas in Financial Arrangements	51
4.6.	Potential Benefits of PPP Ideas for Financial Arrangements	53

SUMMARY

A primary component of U.S. military strategy is to achieve military advantage through technological superiority. Maintaining technological superiority is expensive, and the continuing decline of the Army's science and technology (S&T) budget and the planned restructuring of laboratory, research, development, and test facilities[1] will make it more challenging than ever for the Army to achieve this goal. Moreover, the recently proposed Base Realignment and Closure (BRAC) actions[2] pose additional challenges to the Army's ability to carry out its military mission.

To meet these formidable challenges, the Army must find innovative ways to conduct its research to maintain technological superiority and explore concepts that can optimize infrastructure utilization. A public-private partnership (PPP) is a promising innovative approach that can help the Army achieve its research goals and meet its infrastructure challenges. As we will show, the Army has already used some forms of PPP, but it has not aggressively exploited their use in all the forms and variants now available.

In this report a PPP is defined as a collaborative arrangement between the government and one or more private parties. By combining government expertise, assets, and resources with complementary contributions from the private sector, PPPs can offer the Army op-

---

[1] Report to Congress, *Vision 21: The Plan for 21st Century Laboratories and Test and Evaluation Centers of the Department of Defense*, April 30, 1996.

[2] *Report of the Quadrennial Defense Review*, William S. Cohen, Secretary of Defense, Department of Defense, May 1997, pp. viii–ix.

portunities to leverage its resources, create new assets, increase the value of existing assets, and generate a revenue stream. As an alternative to sale or BRAC, PPPs also can improve the Army's ability to do leading-edge research by retaining self-supporting research installations that would otherwise be permanently lost. It is important to appreciate that PPPs are not defensive actions in the way that many Army actions have been (downsizing, cutbacks, etc.).

THE COMPLEMENTARY CONTRIBUTIONS IN PUBLIC-PRIVATE PARTNERSHIPS

A key strength of PPPs is that the participants make complementary contributions to compose a package that makes good business sense and offers benefits to all parties. The Army's contributions to infrastructure PPPs are likely to involve its vast holdings of property, buildings, other tangible assets such as equipment and specialized areas such as disposal facilities, and the systems that govern their operation. In the area of intellectual property, Army contributions are likely to be scientific expertise, patents, databases, and other elements of its knowledge base. Financial arrangement PPPs involving the Army will most likely center around accomplishing a specific Army objective and may be tied to elements of its infrastructure and intellectual property assets.

Private firms are likely to contribute to PPPs with marketing expertise, access to capital, access to leading-edge technology, and operating expertise. Marketing is the art of selling a product or service. It usually involves combining product/service use analysis with pricing, promotion, place, and targeted consumers. Access to capital means access to money. In this case, the money would be used to help finance a collaborative effort. Access to leading-edge technology means that the most modern technology will be used in research efforts to advance the state of the art. Operating expertise is the know-how to manage land and/or facilities efficiently.

THE TREND TOWARD INCREASED USE OF PUBLIC-PRIVATE PARTNERSHIPS

The government, and the military in particular, has begun to recognize the benefits of private-sector PPP contributions. Evidence of this recognition is provided by a number of legislative changes and government actions that together have created an environment more conducive to PPPs.

Legislative Change

Barriers that once kept the government and industry from collaborating have steadily been reduced through legislation. The legislative changes have made it much easier and more lucrative for the military to enter into PPPs. Before the 1980s, the accepted means of procuring needed military equipment and services was a standard contract. Contracts required adherence to very strict guidance under the Federal Acquisition Regulation (FAR) and the Defense Federal Acquisition Regulation Supplement (DFARS). The regulations proved to be too restrictive to attract many companies to do business with the government. But over the past two decades, legislative actions have introduced new contractual vehicles in which the adherence to some DoD regulations are eased or eliminated. Cooperative Research and Development Agreements (CRADAs), Cooperative Agreements (CAs), and Other Transactions (OTs) are some of these newer vehicles.[3] By affording the flexibility to tailor agreements to meet the needs of all parties, they have increased the military's ability to collaborate with commercial entities and enter into PPPs.

Other legislative actions extended the military's authority to enter into agreements with commercial entities that want to conduct commercial test and evaluation activities at military facilities. Legislation has been amended to promote an increase in the use of partnership ventures between the private sector and the government, while attracting more nontraditional government contractors to enhance the flow of technology.

Continuing this trend, the recent Technology Transfer Commercialization Act aims to encourage technology transfers to the private sector by simplifying licensing procedures for federally owned inventions. Proposed changes are also being considered for 10 USC

---

[3]Title 10, United States Code, Section 2371, "Advanced Research Projects: Transactions Other Than Contracts and Grants."

§2667,[4] the primary vehicle for leveraging fixed assets. The proposed changes will significantly increase the attractiveness of infrastructure PPPs that include leasing.

Actions by Organizations Within the Department of Defense

Recent actions by various organizations in the Department of Defense continue to improve the climate for using PPPs. For example, the Quadrennial Defense Review (QDR) emphasized the need to reengineer the DoD's infrastructure and business practices through a "Revolution in Business Affairs" (RBA). Many RBA tenets are consistent with the objectives of PPPs. In addition, the National Defense Panel (NDP) was tasked to assess the Quadrennial Defense Review, and it isolated "infrastructure" and "science and technology"[5] as special issues that needed to be integrated with its development of QDR alternatives. Major emphasis was placed on maintaining technological superiority.[6] The notion of exploiting the efficiency and cost-effectiveness of the commercial sector, especially in high technology, is a key element of this issue, and PPPs provide a good means for doing this. Finally, recent Defense Science Board (DSB) studies[7] have also made recommendations that are consistent with using PPPs. The studies expound the need for efficiencies, initiatives, and innovations—all the things that PPPs inherently encourage.

Activities at the Local Government Level

At the local/state government level, there is a groundswell of PPP activities involving developers. More and more public agencies, uni-

---

[4]Title 10, United States Code, Section 2667, "Leases: Non-Excess Property."

[5]"NDP Sees 14 'Special Issues' in Developing ADR Alternatives," *Inside the Army*, July 12, 1997, p. 9.

[6]Emile Ettedgui, private communication, August 1997.

[7]*Report of the Defense Science Board 1996 Summer Study on Achieving an Innovative Support Structure for 21st Century Military Superiority: Higher Performance at Lower Costs*, Washington, D.C.: Defense Science Board, November 1996. *Report of the Defense Science Board Task Force on Defense Acquisition Reform (Phase III): A Streamlined Approach to Weapons Systems Research, Development and Acquisition: The Application of Commercial Practices*, Washington, D.C.: Defense Science Board, May 1996.

Summary xvii

versities, and school districts are teaming up with developers to plan, finance, and develop a range of projects—from office buildings, hotels, and entertainment/retail centers to convention centers, correctional facilities, sports facilities, and housing. The annual volume of construction of new public/private developments will reach $22 billion this year. This volume is expected to expand to $25 to $30 billion next year.[8] This continued growth at the local level can be expected to spur other government agencies, such as the Army, to engage in more PPPs in the future.

A PROJECTED EVALUATION OF PUBLIC-PRIVATE PARTNERSHIPS

As Army use of PPPs grows, more and more innovation is also likely to accommodate the variety of situations in which PPPs will be applied. Some innovations, such as fee-for-use of equipment or infrastructure, becoming a third party in established programs, and negotiating discounts, will be extensions of practices already being tried by various military services. Other new PPP ideas can be borrowed from the academic and commercial worlds.

Clearly, there is a wide range of possible PPP innovations. The Army needs to be able to evaluate the novel PPP concepts with respect to their feasibility and the benefits they can be expected to bring. In this report we describe a first-order screening tool to determine the likely benefits of each idea. We also present a screening tool for gaining a first-order indication of feasibility. Table S.1 lists the feasibility criteria and the benefits criteria that make up our screening tools. The Army can use these tools to winnow lists of ideas down to ones that it may want to look into in more detail.

CLOSING REMARKS

Before the Army can consider expanding its participation in PPPs, it must first have a good understanding of which ideas are feasible with respect to what the Army can contribute. The Army must determine

---

[8]John Stainback, "Advantages of Public/Private Development Partnerships," *Urban Land*, July 1997, pp. 24–27 and 60–64.

Table S.1

Evaluation Criteria

Feasibility Criteria	Potential Benefits Criteria
Legality	Leverage/reduce cost
Acceptance	Increase value
Attractiveness	Create new capabilities/assets Influence technology early on Improve readiness posture Generate revenue

which of its properties are underutilized, which assets have excess capacity, and what intellectual property it owns. Such an internal accounting would allow the Army to develop the ideas in this report with its specific contribution in mind. Once the Army has identified its candidate contributions, it must proactively look for interested private partners. Although PPPs should be beneficial to all parties, a considerable amount of time and energy could be expended to fashion one that is agreeable to the Army and its private partner(s).

Some Army Materiel Command (AMC) personnel have raised the concern that PPPs that generate revenue provide opportunities to reduce budgets by the amount of revenue generated. Clearly, the legislative trends and actions by government agencies are aimed at encouraging PPPs, while budget reductions would do the opposite. This concern can be alleviated by making sure that those making budget decisions are aware of the utility of PPPs and understand how budget decisions affect the realization of that utility. In this respect, regulatory guidance may be appropriate. Alternatively, revenue-generating PPPs can be fashioned so that the Army's return comes in in-kind payments rather than cash payments.

This report shows that PPPs can return benefits to the Army that may not be possible with other types of agreements. The Army can use PPPs to optimize the utility of excess capacity infrastructure and its store of intellectual property. Moreover, recent government actions encourage the use of PPPs, and although the Army has begun to use these collaborative agreements, PPPs are still a largely untapped approach. We encourage the Army to exploit the range of opportunities PPPs offer to help it meet its military needs, and we recommend that proposed PPP ideas be examined using the screening method presented in this report.

ACKNOWLEDGMENTS

The authors wish to thank Richard Montgomery, RAND consultant, for proposing and developing the equity fund concept; John Stainback, Ernst & Young, for sharing his thoughts on public-private development ventures; James D. Harper, Jr., President, JDH Realty Company, for providing useful information and insights on development ventures; John Masterman, LaSalle Partners, for discussing financial agreements; and Lieutenant General (ret.) Vince Russo, for reviewing some of the revenue-generation concepts. In addition, we would like to thank Barbara Kenny for preparing the charts and typing the manuscript. For their thorough and insightful reviews of this document, we thank Richard Wright, RAND Contracts and Grants Office; Jack Borsting, University of Southern California School of Business; and Paul Bracken, Yale University School of Organization and Management.

For their valuable inputs and suggestions, special thanks go to Michael Fisette, Principal Deputy for Technology; Colonel Robert Filbey, Garrison Commander, Yuma Proving Ground; Alan King, Executive Assistant, Yuma Proving Ground; Colonel Earle Richardson, Deputy Chief of Staff for Housing, Engineering, Environment, and Installation Logistics, HQ AMC; William Medsger, HQ AMC General Counsel; William Auger, HQ AMC; Suzanne Carlton, Management Analyst, Office of the Chief of Staff of the Army; Sharon Weinhold, Budget Analyst, Assistant Secretary of the Army for Financial Management; Pat Woznick, Contracting Officer, Intelligence Center and School; Richard Dunn, General Counsel, DARPA; Al Antelman, Engineer, Port Hueneme Naval Station; and Christina Kennedy, Defense Contracts Management Command (Seattle). Finally, the information that Monica Shephard, Deputy Director for Shore Operations, and her staff provided on the Norfolk Naval Station activities is greatly appreciated.

ACRONYMS

AMC	Army Materiel Command
ARMS	Armament Retooling and Manufacturing Support
ASA(FM&C)	Assistant Secretary of the Army for Financial Management and Comptroller
BRAC	Base Realignment and Closure
CA	Cooperative Agreement
CECOM	Communications-Electronics Command
CRADA	Cooperative Research and Development Agreement
CRAF	Civil Reserve Air Fleet
DARPA	Defense Advanced Research Projects Agency
DCMC	Defense Contract Management Command
DFARS	Defense Federal Acquisition Regulation Supplement
DoDGARs	Department of Defense Grant and Agreement Regulations
DSB	Defense Science Board
ERIM	Environmental Research Institute of Michigan
FAR	Federal Acquisition Regulation
FTTA	Federal Technology Transfer Act

HHMMT	Hand-Held Multi-Media Terminals
HR	House of Representatives
HRP	Hudson River Partners
NDP	National Defense Panel
NTTAA	National Technology Transfer and Advancement Act
OT	Other Transaction
PAA	Post Award Authority
PAT	Process Action Team
PLA	Patent License Agreement
PPP	Public-Private Partnership
QDR	Quadrennial Defense Review
RBA	Revolution in Business Affairs
R&D	Research and Development
RDEC	Research, Development, and Engineering Center
RTTC	Regional Technology Transfer Centers
S&T	Science and Technology
SAFM	Office of the Assistant Secretary of the Army for Financial Management and Comptroller
SBIR	Small Business Innovation Research
SGI	Silicon Graphics, Inc.
TOA	Total Obligational Authority
TTCA	Technology Transfer Commercialization Act
USC	United States Code
YPG	Yuma Proving Ground

Chapter One

INTRODUCTION

A primary component of U.S. military strategy is to achieve military advantage through technological superiority. Maintaining technological superiority is expensive, and the continuing decline of the Army's science and technology (S&T) budget and the recently announced restructuring of laboratory, research, development, and test facilities[1] will make it more challenging than ever for the Army to achieve this goal. Moreover, the recently announced Base Realignment and Closure (BRAC) actions[2] pose additional challenges to the Army's ability to carry out its military mission; BRAC will reduce the Army's infrastructure, forcing it to rethink its strategies for maintaining the flexibility it needs to uphold its readiness posture.

To meet these formidable challenges, the Army must seek innovative ways to conduct its R&D to maintain technological superiority and explore concepts that can optimize infrastructure utilization. A public-private partnership (PPP) is a promising innovative approach that can help the Army achieve its research goals in its new, smaller restructured R&D environment. As we will show, although the Army has used PPPs in the past (as demonstrated by some of the examples we will present), it has not aggressively exploited their use in all the forms and variants now available.

---

[1] Report to Congress, *Vision 21: The Plan for 21st Century Laboratories and Test and Evaluation Centers of the Department of Defense*, April 30, 1996.

[2] *Report of the Quadrennial Defense Review*, William S. Cohen, Secretary of Defense, May 1997, p. viii.

DEFINITION OF PUBLIC-PRIVATE PARTNERSHIP

For the purposes of this report, a PPP is defined as a collaborative arrangement between the government and one or more private parties. PPPs specify joint rights and responsibilities, which implies some sharing of risks, costs, or assets. In a PPP, there is mutual leveraging of each partner's strengths, and the resulting synergy coupled with close cooperation allows all parties to effectively achieve common goals.

The ideal PPP proceeds in a cooperative spirit that arises out of mutual trust, the combining of complementary assets, and shared objectives. In this vein, a PPP is distinctive from more common ways of conducting government business; in traditional contracts, for example, there is no leveraging of private-sector expertise or resources. A PPP is also different from outsourcing, in which the government is essentially the buyer and the supplier is the seller. However, outsourcing agreements now often include elements of PPPs in them. A recent outsourcing agreement between the state of Connecticut and IBM for data processing included provisions for state officials to have access to IBM's new electronic commerce institute. The idea behind this was to introduce electronic commerce to state government operations, e.g., allowing residents to renew automobile registration over the Internet. In exchange for the outsourcing contract, IBM is to educate state officials on electronic commerce. The cost to IBM is low, and the benefit to the state is considerable.

BENEFITS OF PUBLIC-PRIVATE PARTNERSHIPS

By combining government expertise, assets, and resources with complementary contributions from the private sector, PPPs can offer a variety of benefits. For the Army, PPP benefits include opportunities to

- leverage its assets, reduce capital investments, reduce costs, or decrease outlays to achieve infrastructure, intellectual property, or financial arrangement goals;
- increase the value of its property or other assets;
- create new capabilities or assets that help the Army accomplish its military mission;

- influence technology early and thereby get equipment fielded earlier and/or possibly at lower cost;
- improve its readiness posture; and
- receive a stream of revenue to fund projects that help the Army accomplish its military mission.

In the remainder of this section, we present examples that illustrate how each benefit can be the result of a PPP.

Leverage Assets, Reduce Costs, or Decrease Outlays

PPPs can give the Army opportunities to leverage its assets more efficiently. For example, a PPP that incorporates cost sharing allows the Army to accomplish goals with less funds than traditional contractual or outsourcing arrangements would require. Since both Army and private partner funds are being spent to accomplish the same goals, the PPP arrangement dictates a collaborative relationship. For example, the Communications-Electronics Command (CECOM) and ITT (Aerospace Communications Division) have a cooperative agreement (CA) to demonstrate a network of Hand-Held Multi-Media Terminals (HHMMT) that can transfer voice, data, and video in a multihop environment for both defense and industrial applications. The HHMMT will provide the military with a wireless, portable communication system capable of transferring vital command-and-control information on the battlefield while the forces are moving. At the same time, the HHMMT concept may culminate in a series of hand-held commercial electronic devices with various applications (e.g., game players, palm-top computers, sophisticated portable graphics/video transmit/receive systems). The total value of this agreement is $3,312,600. The government's share is $1,656,230, half of the cost. ITT is contributing the other half of the project funds, thus allowing CECOM to accomplish its goals at less cost.[3] ITT benefits because some of the development costs of a potential spin-off commercial product are being supported by the government.

---

[3]This agreement was completed pursuant to 10 USC 2371, "Other Transactions," under DARPA and transferred to CECOM. The agreement, no. DAAB07-96-3D760, was finalized on June 11, 1996.

Increase Value of Army Assets

A PPP can also offer the Army an opportunity to increase the value of its assets. For example, the Armament Retooling and Manufacturing Support (ARMS) program was initiated in 1993 to avoid closing Army ammunition plants and to maintain ramp-up production capability after the Cold War.[4] In this program, Congress appropriated $190 million to assist in commercializing some of the plants. The Army Materiel Command (AMC) used the funds to develop strategic reuse and marketing plans, make leasehold improvements, and provide loan guarantees. Facility use contractors are hired to maintain the facilities and manage the leases. Eleven plants are participating in the program. The program is expected to break even in the year 2000 and yield an annual net revenue of $15 million thereafter. In this case, private firms use the facilities for commercial purposes during peacetime. The Army retains ownership of the modernized facilities and can return them to ammunition manufacturing during national emergencies. The ARMS program not only increases the value of an Army asset—the ammunition plants—through modernization and continued maintenance, it also preserves that asset for military use in time of need. Moreover, it gives the private firms commercial facilities at less cost than they would have paid to buy their own land and build from scratch.

Create New Army Capabilities and Assets

A PPP can create new Army capabilities and assets. At the Yuma Proving Ground (YPG), the Army is investigating a PPP with a private firm to develop a hotel on Army property. The private firm would fund the building of the facility and operate it. The Army would receive a percentage of monthly sales and retain ownership of the land and hotel. Hence, in this case, the Army would gain a new asset, a hotel, via the PPP. The private firm would gain profits from operating the hotel. Those on business or visiting the Yuma area would be able to stay in a new modern hotel close to the YPG. In this case, the Army, the private firm, and the public could all benefit if the PPP were executed successfully.

---

[4]"Conversion of Ammunition Plants Offer Once-in-a-Lifetime Opportunity," *News@ARMS*, Issue 1.0, 1996 (a publication of Operation Enterprise, Web site at http://www.openterprise.com).

Early Influence on Technology

A PPP can offer the Army an opportunity to influence technology. By making its requirements known early to industry, the Army has a greater chance of obtaining the military version of equipment more quickly and at less cost. The PPP between CECOM and ITT described above illustrates this point. In this agreement, ITT will develop HHMMTs that may be used by soldiers in the field. The HHMMTs are highly applicable to the Army's military needs, but they also offer immense commercial prospects. In this case, the Army is influencing the HHMMT technology early in the R&D phase and will likely receive the military version shortly after HHMMTs emerge, while a large-volume commercial market is likely to help lower the cost of similar equipment produced for the Army.

Improve Readiness Posture

A PPP can offer the government an alternative to the sale or BRAC of underutilized assets. For example, instead of closing a facility, the government could lease some or all of its plant and/or land to a private company. Funds from the leasing arrangement could be applied toward the infrastructure budget of that facility. If market rates are charged, the installation may be self-sustaining or may even generate enough funds to augment the budgets of other installations. By using a PPP to lease assets, rather than sell or BRAC them, the government can retain control of the assets in the event of an emergency and thereby improve its readiness posture—the facilities are kept clean and modernized and funds are generated to offset expenses. For the government's private partners, the leasing firms may be able to acquire use of facilities at a cost lower than that for alternative sites. The partnering firms may also be able to site their operations in a location that would not otherwise be available. Hence, in some cases, using a PPP as an alternative to BRAC or sale of government assets can be a win-win situation for the government as well as its partners.

The Long Beach Naval Station illustrates some of the ideas about how PPPs could have been used as an alternative to BRAC. The Long Beach Naval Station consists of approximately 400 acres of land and is being transferred to the Long Beach Port Authority via BRAC in

1997. In the interim, the Navy is leasing sixteen acres of underutilized land to the port authority for approximately $50,000 per acre per year (approximately $800,000 rent per year). If this base were not scheduled for closure, the Navy, arguably, could have generated at least $800,000 per year for the sixteen acres it is now leasing to the port authority. If just 10 percent of the facility (i.e., 40 acres) were leased at the $50,000 per acre per year rate, the Navy could have generated $2 million per year to offset the base's infrastructure cost and keep the facility available for use in the case of a national security emergency. This illustration suggests that in some instances, the government might use a PPP as an alternative to BRAC.

Generate Revenue

A PPP can also generate revenue for Army uses. For example, the Army has entered into a CRADA with a private firm to jointly research the properties and uses of spider silk.[5] This PPP specifies that the Army will receive a percentage of the royalties from any patent that results from the joint research effort, regardless of who owns the patent. If a major breakthrough occurs, then this PPP represents a revenue-generation potential for funds that can be used for future Army research efforts.

OBJECTIVE AND SCOPE

At the request of Army Materiel Command, the Arroyo Center was asked to create a strategy for managing the development of advanced technologies with special attention to the changing environment under which research and development must be conducted in the future. In the initial phase of this research, we showed that significant opportunities exist for the Army to more effectively achieve its R&D goals through collaboration with industry.[6] In the second phase of the research, we investigated new concepts the Army could use to implement a collaborative R&D policy and showed how effective the

---

[5]Phillip Brandler, Director, U.S. Army Natick Research, Development and Engineering Center, private communication, September 1997.

[6]Carolyn Wong, *An Analysis of Collaborative Research Opportunities in the Army*, Santa Monica, CA: RAND, MR-675-A, 1998.

concepts would be in attracting nontraditional military suppliers into research collaborations with the Army.[7] In the research described here, we expand on the notion of a collaborative research strategy and discuss the evolving use of PPPs in the management and development of infrastructure, intellectual property, and financial arrangements.

Clearly, a PPP requires one or more commercial firms as the Army's partner, and commercial firms will consider partnering only when there is a match in goals and a potential for profit for the private partner. Hence, we have limited our consideration of PPPs in the infrastructure area to include the management and development of land, assets, buildings, and the systems that govern their operation when these components can yield a commercial benefit.

The scope of our study in the intellectual property area includes R&D in the technologies that are of interest to the Army and that might have some application to a commercial product or service as well as assets such as scientific expertise and know-how, patents, and databases.[8] For example, studies to determine warfare strategy to accomplish the Army's combat mission would not be PPP candidates, but R&D in computer sciences would be.

We included financial arrangements in our study because the Army does not have any collaborative efforts in this area and there is considerable potential for the Army to reap some of the PPP benefits through financial arrangements.

BACKGROUND

The Army must maintain its technological edge while facing constraints imposed by reductions in S&T funding. As shown in Figure 1.1, the combined budget for basic research, exploratory development, and advanced technology development has declined over the past fifteen years. While there have been ups and downs in the S&T

---

[7]See Kenneth Horn, Elliot Axelband, Ike Chang, Paul Steinberg, Carolyn Wong, and Howell Yee, *Performing Collaborative Research with Nontraditional Military Suppliers*, Santa Monica, CA: RAND, MR-830-A, 1997.

[8]See Wong, *An Analysis of Collaborative Research Opportunities in the Army*, op. cit., for a description of dual-use technologies.

budget line, the general trend has been downward, and this downward trend is projected to continue in the future.[9] Budget estimates out to fiscal year 2003 show a continuing decline in dollars, albeit not as sharp a decline as that experienced in the mid-1990s.[10] Even so, by fiscal year 2003, the Army's S&T budget will be about $1.1 billion, or roughly half of what it was in fiscal year 1993. In light of these budget realities, the Army must modify its approach to achieving its R&D goals or risk losing its ability to conduct leading-edge research.

While Army funds for research and development have been declining and are not expected to grow during the next five years, those of the

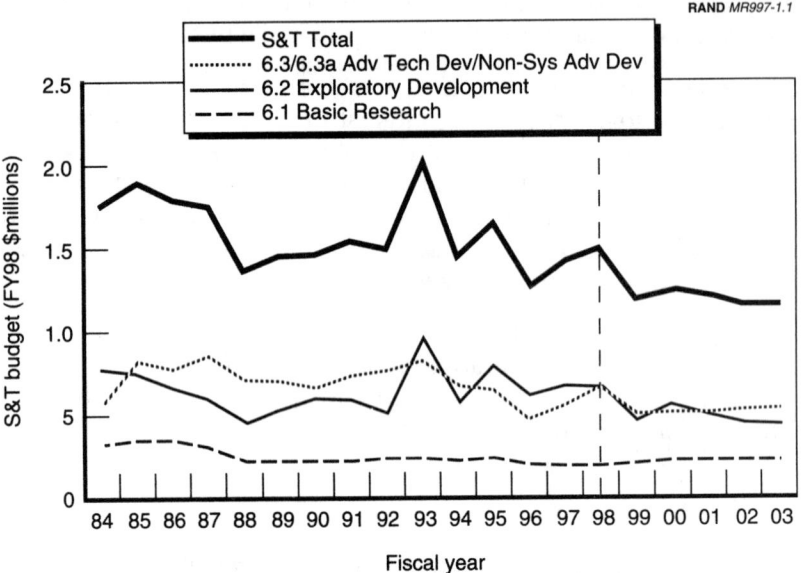

NOTE: FY84–97=actuals; FY98–FY03=proposed.

Figure 1.1—Army Research Budget for Fiscal Years 1984–2003

---

[9]Calculated from data provided by the ASA (FM&C) (Assistant Secretary of the Army for Financial Management and Comptroller) and deflators shown in Table 5.5 of Office of the Under Secretary of Defense (Comptroller), *National Defense Budget Estimates for FY98*, Washington, D.C.: Department of Defense, March 1997, p. 53.

[10]John Carey, "What Price Science?" *Business Week*, May 26, 1997, pp. 166–170.

private sector have been steady or slightly growing since 1990. Private corporations are expected to increase overall research and development spending 6 percent in 1997 to approximately $120 billion (FY97 dollars).[11]

A comparison of the absolute dollars spent on research shows that private industry spent significantly more money on research than the Army has spent. The private sector's spending on research is approximately one hundred times greater than the Army's research budget. Of course, only some of the specific research performed with private-sector funds is of interest to the Army. But even if only 1 percent of the private sector's annual research funds are spent on research of interest to the Army, that figure rivals the Army's entire annual research budget. The relatively larger and nondecreasing research spending indicates that the private sector has or can access the resources to fund or help fund research that is of interest to it and to the Army.

Our previous research has shown that the Army has significant opportunities to more effectively achieve its R&D goals through collaboration with the private sector.[12] We have also shown how the Army can effectively implement a collaborative R&D policy.[13] The discussion above shows that the private sector has the financial means to perform collaborative research with the Army. In addition, PPPs can benefit the Army by creating opportunities for it to leverage its resources, creating new assets or increasing the value of existing assets, or generating a revenue stream. PPPs also improve the Army's ability to do leading-edge research by retaining self-supporting research installations that would under BRAC/sell be permanently lost to the Army. In short, PPPs can be used to accomplish many Army military objectives. In this report, we will specifically examine how PPPs can help the Army gain benefits through infrastructure, intellectual property, and financial arrangements.

---

[11]Ibid.

[12]Horn et al., *Performing Collaborative Research with Nontraditional Military Suppliers*, op. cit.

[13]Wong, *An Analysis of Collaborative Research Opportunities in the Army*, op. cit.

ORGANIZATION

Chapter Two describes how private-party contributions can complement the Army's contributions to PPPs. Chapter Three discusses recent legislative and government trends indicating that the government is likely to enter into more PPPs in the future. Chapter Four extrapolates from the trends and presents a projection of how Army use of PPPs might evolve in the future. Chapter Five presents closing remarks and recommendations. Appendix A contains detailed descriptions of the specific ideas presented in Chapter Four. Appendix B contains a listing of the examples used throughout this report to illustrate points, concepts, and approaches.

Chapter Two

THE COMPLEMENTARY CONTRIBUTIONS IN PUBLIC-PRIVATE PARTNERSHIPS

ARMY CONTRIBUTIONS

One of the primary characteristics of PPPs is that the participants make complementary contributions that together compose a package that makes good business sense and offers benefits to all parties. In the case of the Army, its contributions to infrastructure PPPs are likely to involve its vast holdings of property, buildings, other tangible assets such as equipment and specialized areas such as disposal facilities, and the systems that govern their operation. Other government holdings that might be offered include access to restricted zones, passage through restricted areas, use of restricted airspace, and sharing of communications bandwidth. In the intellectual property area, Army contributions are likely to be scientific expertise, patents, databases, and other elements of its knowledge base. Financial arrangement PPPs involving the Army will most likely be centered around accomplishing a specific Army objective and may be tied to elements of its infrastructure and intellectual property assets.[1]

PRIVATE-SECTOR CONTRIBUTIONS

Among the elements that private firms are likely to contribute to an infrastructure PPP are marketing expertise, access to capital, and operating expertise. In an intellectual property PPP, the private sector

---

[1]The Army does not have any financial PPPs. PPPs that are financial arrangements will be discussed in more detail in Chapter Four.

is still likely to contribute marketing expertise and access to capital, but instead of operating expertise, it may contribute access to leading-edge technology. In financial arrangement PPPs, the private sector contributions are likely to be marketing expertise and access to capital.

Below, we present definitions and illustrations of the elements that the private sector is likely to contribute to PPPs, highlighting the differences and similarities between infrastructure, intellectual property, and financial arrangement PPPs.[2]

Marketing Expertise

Marketing/marketing research expertise is the art of selling a product or service. Marketing/marketing expertise usually involves combining analysis of product/service uses with pricing, promotion, place, and targeted consumers. Marketing expertise can be applicable to PPPs in the infrastructure, intellectual property, and financial arrangement areas.

The private sector has extensive experience and expertise in marketing. A company's fortunes are often directly tied to how successfully it markets its newly developed products/services. A commercial company makes its profits from sales of its products and services, and the higher the sales volume, the higher the company's profits are likely to be. Hence, the private sector usually devotes considerable resources to the marketing aspect of its business. Whereas the Army sees technology as a product, the private sector sees it as one piece of a large value-added chain of interdependent activities. Changing one piece of the chain has impacts on the rest of the chain. For example, the graphical user interface for computers was not merely a better piece of software—it had revolutionary impacts on who used computers and how they were used. Recognizing such impacts is a skill much more prevalent in business than in the Army. Only by

---

[2]Other elements such as operational flexibility, financial expertise, legal expertise, and managerial expertise can also be pivotal private-sector contributions, but these contributions are likely to be applicable to specific instances rather than generally appropriate to most PPPs.

working with the private sector can the Army understand the value of the technologies that it does possess—and their market potential.[3]

The Army's infrastructure exists for military purposes. The Army will attempt to extract PPP benefits from its infrastructure if it can be done without interference with military uses. But as a general rule, the Army does not inventory its infrastructure assets for the purpose of extracting their commercial value. Thus, the Army does not proactively market its infrastructure assets because that is not part of its mission. Hence, the Army has limited experience in infrastructure marketing; in an infrastructure PPP, it makes sense for the Army to look to its private-sector partner for marketing expertise.

Army research is usually directly related to its military mission. Although the Army will commercialize dual-use intellectual property, it does not perform R&D with commercialization in mind and thus has little expertise in marketing R&D products. The Army can benefit from expert marketing of its R&D products because successful commercialization of a product or service generally lowers its purchase price. Therefore, the Army can financially benefit by looking to the private sector to contribute marketing expertise in collaborative R&D efforts.

The Defense Advanced Research Projects Agency's (DARPA) Other Transaction (OT) agreement with Environmental Research Institute of Michigan (ERIM) illustrates how the government looked to a private firm for marketing expertise.[4] In this agreement, DARPA grants ERIM radar imaging technology, and ERIM and its partner commercialize the technology for government and nongovernment uses. DARPA, in return will receive royalties from commercial sales.

The Army does not have any PPPs that are financial arrangements, such as credit cards or venture capital funds. The marketing function that makes such arrangements successful can be carried out by the private sector. If the Army were to consider financial arrange-

---

[3] Roger E. Levian, *Taking Technology to Market*, Menlo Park, CA: Crisp Publications, 1997.

[4] Office of the Assistant Secretary of Defense (Public Affairs), News Release, Ref. No. 063-97, February 1, 1997.

ment PPPs, it should look to its private-sector partner for marketing expertise.

Access to Capital

Access to capital often means access to financing. In this case, the money would be used to help finance a collaborative effort. Access to capital is relevant to infrastructure, intellectual property, and financial arrangement PPPs.

The private sector often borrows money to finance its business expenses. Business expenses could include the expansion of a company's infrastructure, the development of intellectual property, or the launching of a new financial arrangement. A firm may enjoy excellent credit with one or more financial institutions that can extend loans to the company. These factors indicate that the private sector may have access to capital that could be applied toward collaborative efforts that benefit the Army.

The amount the Army can spend on infrastructure is limited each year by its budget. The Army does not borrow money for infrastructure needs. Hence, the Army does not have the experience or the legal authority to access capital beyond its budgetary constraints. Therefore, in infrastructure PPPs, the Army should look to its private-sector partner for at least some of the collaborative effort funds.

The Army's S&T budget has been decreasing and is likely to continue to decline. In addition, the Army funds its R&D based on the size of its budget. The Army does not borrow money to fund any project beyond what budget funds will provide for, regardless of how advantageous the project may seem. So the Army has only one source of R&D funds, and the level of those funds is often inadequate to pay for all the research the Army needs to reach its R&D goals. One way for the Army to leverage its R&D dollars is to enter into collaborative efforts with leading-edge firms that have access to capital and share in the funding of dual-use research.[5]

---

[5]See Horn et al., *Performing Collaborative Research with Nontraditional Military Suppliers,* op. cit., for a discussion of how the Army can attract leading-edge firms that have not traditionally done business with the Army.

The Fort Drum Housing Development is an example of how the private sector's access to capital can help finance partnerships that benefit both the Army and its partners.[6] Another example is the development of a hot weather auto test center at the Army's Yuma Proving Ground (YPG). This concept was approved in February 1997 by the Army and proposes that YPG partner with a vehicle manufacturer to build the auto test center. If successful, the private partner would fund the construction of the test courses in exchange for the value of a long-term lease. YPG will provide utilities and sell test and test-support services to the facility on a cost-reimbursable basis. The vehicle manufacturer will benefit via the long-term lease. The Army will gain expanded capability to test military vehicles without investing its own funds.

Access to Leading-Edge Technology

Access to leading-edge technology ensures that the most modern technology will be used in research efforts to advance the state of the art. Access to leading-edge technology is an advantage that can be leveraged by intellectual property PPPs.

The private sector holds the lead in many technologies that are of Army interest. Examples include textiles and information technologies such as telecommunications. Research units at commercial firms are usually aware of the latest technical developments in their field, have the most advanced equipment to conduct R&D, and are cognizant of what their competitors are researching.

In contrast, the Army is often not aware of the latest developments in certain fields, doesn't always have access to the most advanced equipment, and doesn't have the time or resources to keep current on private-sector R&D efforts. Through PPPs, the Army can gain better access to the entire body of private-sector knowledge, equipment, and know-how without investing additional dollars to gain it. Clearly, in dual-use fields where the private sector holds the technological lead, it makes sense for the Army to look to its private partner to provide access to leading-edge technology.

---

[6]See Appendix B for more discussion about the Fort Drum Housing Development.

The Army's Cooperative Research and Development Agreement (CRADA) with Silicon Graphics, Inc. (SGI) is an example of an agreement in which the private sector is providing the Army with access to leading-edge technology. In this agreement, SGI will work with the Army to research simulation capabilities for dismounted soldiers and the rest of the combined arms force.[7] SGI has the simulation expertise and the computer technology needed by the Army to effectively process and analyze information. The agreement calls for an exchange of technology and the protection of all intellectual property, but no monetary exchange. Through this CRADA, the Army will reap some of the benefits of SGI's investment in R&D. SGI will gain insights into Army computing requirements, allowing SGI to structure its computers to accommodate that need.

Operating Expertise

Operating expertise is the know-how to manage a facility efficiently. Operating expertise is relevant to many infrastructure PPPs.

The private sector operates facilities in hopes of attracting customers and thereby maximizing its profit from them. Hence, the private sector tends to have experience in establishing policies and procedures that will help it do so. The private sector must obey all laws that are applicable but is otherwise unrestricted in how it operates a facility.

The Army operates many facilities, some of which may be in the same business category as a commercial facility (e.g., a hotel). In the overlapping areas, the Army operates these facilities for the benefit of soldiers, not to make a profit. As such, the Army may focus more on just providing the required services rather than establishing an efficient and attractive operation. The Army may also be further constrained in how a facility is run—government regulations that are not applicable to the private sector (e.g., DoD regulations) may be applicable to the Army. As such, the Army may not have the legal flexibility to operate a facility as a private company could. Hence, in an infrastructure PPP, the private sector can often contribute operating expertise and flexibility.

---

[7] *Inside the Army*, Vol. 8, No. 42, October 21, 1996, p. 1.

The Thayer Hotel at West Point is an example in which the private sector is scheduled to contribute operating expertise in a PPP. For many years, the Thayer Hotel has been owned and operated by the government. The government entered into an agreement with Hudson River Partners (HRP) in 1998. Under the agreement, HRP will take over the hotel from the Army under the terms of a 50-year lease. HRP will renovate the hotel, operate it during the lease term, add a state-of-the-art conference facility, and collect all sales receipts. All costs for these activities will be incurred by HRP. The Army will benefit by the availability of a totally renovated and improved facility on the installation, the receipt of 1 percent of gross sales each quarter, and resumption of control of an improved facility at the end of the lease.

Chapter Three

THE TREND TOWARD INCREASED USE OF PUBLIC-PRIVATE PARTNERSHIPS

In Chapter Two we examined complementary elements that the Army and the private sector are likely to contribute to a PPP and detailed how the Army could benefit from such contributions. The government, and the Army in particular, has begun to recognize the beneficial returns from private-sector PPP contributions. Evidence of this recognition is provided by a number of legislative changes and government actions that together have created an environment more conducive to PPPs.[1] In this chapter we chronicle major legislative changes and actions by various government agencies that have produced a more PPP-friendly environment for the military. In addition, we discuss how the use of PPPs by local governments is not only helping to set the trend for more PPPs at the federal level but is providing momentum to push federal agencies such as the Army toward using more PPPs in the future.

LEGISLATIVE CHANGES

Barriers that previously kept the government and industry from collaborating have steadily been reduced through legislation. The legislative changes have made it much easier and more lucrative for the military to enter into PPPs. Prior to the 1980s, the accepted means of procuring military equipment and services was a standard contract. Contracts required adherence to very strict guidance under

---

[1] It is interesting to note that while various organizations within the DoD are taking actions that are more conducive to PPPs, none of these actions alone explicitly directs the use of PPPs in the future.

the Federal Acquisition Regulation (FAR) and the Defense Federal Acquisition Regulation Supplement (DFARS). These regulations proved too restrictive to attract many companies to do business with the government. Over the past two decades, legislative actions have introduced new instruments in which the adherence to some DoD regulations has been eased or eliminated. Cooperative Research and Development Agreements (CRADAs), Cooperative Agreements (CAs), and Other Transactions (OTs) are some of these newer instruments. They have increased the military's ability to collaborate with commercial entities and enter into PPPs. With the newer instruments, the military has had the flexibility to tailor agreements to meet the needs of all parties.

Figure 3.1 shows a timeline of major legislative actions that have steadily helped to create an environment conducive to PPPs. Below we briefly discuss the most influential pieces of legislation.

Stevenson-Wydler Technology Innovation Act of 1980

Although not an instrument to contract for goods and services, the Stevenson-Wydler Act[2] authorized all federal laboratories to take an active role in transferring federally funded technologies to nongovernment entities. The legislation was an attempt to ensure full use of the government's investment in research and development, and it opened the door for further transfer of government technology that may have potential use in commercial applications. This transfer of technology outside the government served as a means to bring the military and commercial entities together for more than just standard contractual relationships.

Grants

In the 1980s, grants became another method of procuring needed military research. Outlined in 10 USC §2358,[3] grants are usually limited to universities and other nonprofit organizations for research on weapons and other military needs, or for projects of potential in-

___

[2]Codified under Title 15, United States Code, Sections 3701–3714.
[3]Title 10, United States Code, Section 2358, "Research and Development Projects."

The Trend Toward Increased Use of Public-Private Partnerships   21

RAND MR997-3.1

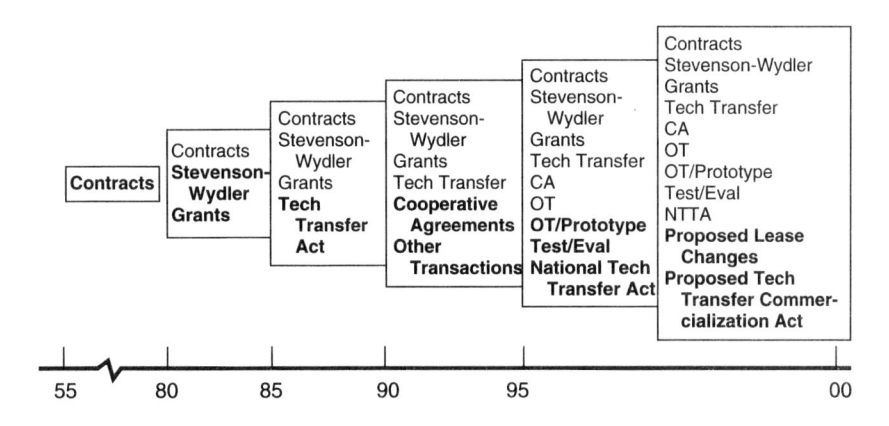

55	80	85	90	95		00
Contracts	Contracts Stevenson- Wydler Grants	Contracts Stevenson- Wydler Grants Tech Transfer Act	Contracts Stevenson- Wydler Grants Tech Transfer Cooperative Agreements Other Transactions	Contracts Stevenson- Wydler Grants Tech Transfer CA OT OT/Prototype Test/Eval National Tech Transfer Act		Contracts Stevenson-Wydler Grants Tech Transfer CA OT OT/Prototype Test/Eval NTTA Proposed Lease Changes Proposed Tech Transfer Commer- cialization Act

Figure 3.1—Timeline of Major Legislative Actions Affecting PPPs

terest to the DoD. But unlike contracts, grants are administered under the Department of Defense Grant and Agreement Regulations (DoDGARs) and do not allow for active government participation in the research. Although the DoDGARs do offer some flexibility, the requirements are still considered burdensome and may discourage the private sector from pursuing DoD grants.

Technology Transfer Act of 1986

The first legislation allowing the military to enter into PPPs was the Federal Technology Transfer Act of 1986 (FTTA). The FTTA allowed federal laboratories to enter into Cooperative Research and Development Agreements (CRADAs) with private industry, universities, and other interested parties. The agreements were limited to research and development projects in which the military could contribute personnel, services, facilities, and all other items necessary for project completion, except funding. The FTTA also allowed for implementation of Patent License Agreements (PLAs), which are designed to protect proprietary information, grant patent rights, and provide for user licenses to industry. In effect, a license is granted to an outside agency to use a government-generated patent. The primary purpose of the FTTA, in allowing for CRADAs and PLAs, is to stimulate the U.S. economy by transferring technology from the military to the commercial sector. Although not intended for the transfer of technology from industry to the military, CRADAs and PLAs were a major improvement in the procurement environment that would eventually make two-way transfer of technology possible.

Cooperative Agreements

In 1989, Congress gave DARPA the authority to use Cooperative Agreements (CAs) under 10 USC §2358[4] and extended their use to all of DoD in 1991. In accordance with Section 2358, CAs can be used for basic research, advanced research, applied research, and development projects that relate to military weapon systems and other needs of potential interest to the DoD. CAs allow cost sharing between the parties. In accordance with 10 USC §2371,[5] more clauses can be added to a CA to authorize a recovery of funds in basic, applied, or advanced research projects. If 10 USC §2371 authority is invoked, the cost-sharing requirement of Section 2371 is also invoked, requiring the military's share not to exceed the total amount provided by other parties.

In addition, CAs, unlike grants, allow for the military to participate in the performance of the research. The ability to share costs, participate in the performance process, and recover funds was a major step forward in furthering the use of PPPs between the military and industry. Even though CAs could not be used where a standard contract is more appropriate, they established the trend away from traditional forms of contracting toward a collaborative relationship as epitomized by PPPs.

Other Transactions

In 1989, 10 USC §2371 gave DARPA the authority to use a form of transaction other than a contract, cooperative agreement, or grant. This authority to use these "Other Transactions" (OTs) was extended

---

[4]Title 10, United States Code, Section 2358, "Research and Development Projects."

[5]Title 10, United States Code, Section 2371, "Advanced Research Projects: Transactions Other Than Contracts and Grants."

to all of DoD in 1991. OTs are not traditional procurement contracts and do not have to adhere to the burdensome guidance of the FAR and DFARS. OTs are also not bound by the provisions of the Bayh-Dole Act. An OT gives the military the freedom to negotiate provisions that are mutually agreeable to the government and the other parties. To the extent practicable, the law requires the government's cost share to be no greater than the sum provided by its partners. In addition, use of OTs is allowed when a standard contract, grant, or CA is not feasible or appropriate. While the authority of the law was not limited to technology base or dual-use projects, the majority of agreements have fallen into this category.

10 USC §2371 created a more flexible instrument for collaboration and was a natural response to the military's demand for easier access to advanced technologies developed in the private sector. Our previous findings indicate that OTs were necessary to attract many of the leading commercial companies that historically avoided government business because of the burdensome and restrictive requirements of the conventional government procurement system.[6] The many benefits of this PPP vehicle, to both the military and industry, warrants increased usage. However, despite the authority to use OTs, the military has embraced their usage on a very limited scale.

Other Transactions for Prototyping

In 1993, Congress amended 10 USC §2371 by adding Section 845 to the existing law. Section 845 allowed DARPA to use OTs for prototype projects.[7] Section 845 was amended in the Fiscal Year 1997 National Defense Authorization Act. The amendment extended Section 845 authority to the military departments and other DoD components. This legislation was another major step forward in the government's ability to form PPPs. The changes expanded the military's flexibility for prototype development by eliminating the need for cost sharing and allowed use of Section 845 OTs even when a standard contract could be used. Additionally, the authority of 845 OTs has

---

[6]See Horn et al., *Performing Collaborative Research with Nontraditional Military Suppliers*, op. cit.

[7]Richard L. Dunn, "Other Applications for 'Other Transactions,'" *Aerospace America*, September 1997.

broadened to projects directly relevant to the development of a weapon or weapon system. This wording can be interpreted broadly to encompass subsystems, components, and technologies; it can even be construed to include training, simulation, and support equipment directly relevant to the "weapon or weapon system." The broad authority could allow for use of an 845 OT in a wide variety of projects. According to Richard Dunn, DARPA's general counsel, "Given the trend toward utilizing off the shelf components and technologies in defense systems, Section 845 prototype projects may often involve the adaptation, testing, or integration of commercial items for military purposes" in the future.[8] As a result, the authority to use 845 OTs for prototyping will open new opportunities for traditional defense contractors to be innovative in their dealings with the DoD, while encouraging nontraditional contractors to do business with the DoD.

Test and Evaluation

In 1993, Congress, under 10 USC §2681,[9] gave the military additional leeway in forming PPPs with outside agencies by extending its authority to enter into contracts with commercial entities that want to conduct commercial test and evaluation activities. Under this legislation, the military can rent test and evaluation facilities to commercial entities to conduct nonmilitary testing. Test and evaluation contracts require the commercial entity to reimburse the military for all direct costs to the government. Such a contract may also include requiring the private party to reimburse the government for indirect costs related to the use of the facilities. This legislation serves not only to enhance the relationship between commercial entities and the military but also increases the utilization of facilities and test equipment, which serves to keep them in working condition.

---

[8]Richard L. Dunn, "Memorandum of Law on Scope of Section 845 Prototype Authority," Arlington, VA: Advanced Research Projects Agency, October 24, 1996.

[9]Title 10, United States Code, Section 2681, "Use of Test Evaluation Installations by Commercial Entities."

National Technology Transfer and Advancement Act of 1995 (NTTAA)

In 1995, the Stevenson-Wydler Technology Innovation Act of 1980 and the Federal Technology Transfer Act of 1986 were amended through the National Technology Transfer and Advancement Act (Public Law 104-113) in an effort to speed commercialization of inventions developed through collaborative agreements between the government and industry. The law provides that under a CRADA, industry partners and the government may have exclusive license rights of new technologies in areas agreed upon during negotiations. The amended law also enhanced incentives for federal employees who develop new inventions or technologies and allows federal laboratories greater flexibility in using royalties that result from commercialization. The changes sought to promote an increase in the use of partnership ventures between the private sector and the government, while attracting more nontraditional government contractors to enhance the flow of technology to government usage. The enhanced incentives for government personnel are intended to encourage creativity in developing new technologies and inventions that may have a government and commercial application.

Proposed Technology Transfer Commercialization Act of 1997 (TTCA)

On September 30, 1997, the TTCA was introduced with the intent of encouraging technology transfers to the private sector by simplifying licensing procedures for federally owned inventions. The bill amends the Stevenson-Wydler Act to "allow Federal laboratories to include already existing patented inventions into a cooperative research and development agreement (CRADA)."[10] The intent of the bill is to increase the incentive for companies to partner with the government by more effectively commercializing on-the-shelf government-owned technologies. The bill also eliminates requirements for a three-month public notification of the availability of an invention for exclusive licensing and an additional two-month

---

[10]Constance A. Morella (8th District, Maryland), "Introductory Statement for H.R. 2544, the Technology Transfer Commercialization Act of 1997."

period for filing of objections once a company responds seeking to license the invention. The notification requirements and the long delay in time-to-market discourages companies from seeking business with the government to commercialize on-the-shelf government inventions. Removing such requirements should accelerate commercialization of government technologies by facilitating CRADAs.[11]

Leases on Non-Excess Property

10 USC §2667[12] is the primary vehicle for leveraging fixed assets. This legislation authorizes the military to lease non-excess property to civilian entities when it is considered advantageous to the government and will promote the national defense or be in the public interest. Rental money received for the lease of non-excess property can be deposited in the Treasury for use by the Army, with no less than 50 percent returned to the installation to directly support the lease, as in facility maintenance and repair or environmental restoration. The money must also be reapportioned by Congress before it is returned to the Army, thus delaying its use for a year. Several limitations, especially the restriction to the installation of 50 percent of the lease receipts and limiting their use to only supporting the lease, significantly reduce the incentive to use this avenue for generating revenue.

Proposed changes to 10 USC §2667 have been reviewed in Army channels and have been forwarded from the Secretary of the Army to the Secretary of Defense for approval and further action.[13] The proposed changes should significantly increase the attractiveness of infrastructure PPPs that include leasing. Under the changes, lease authority would be extended, use of in-kind payments would be expanded, and reapportionment of receipts would be eliminated. The extension of lease authority would allow for the leasing of any

---

[11]With changes in the pending legislation, installations involved in agreements resulting in commercialization of inventions would be allowed to use the royalties in ways seen as appropriate by their commanders, without the added burden of reapportionment and in-kind limitations.

[12]Title 10, United States Code, Section 2667, "Leases: Non-Excess Property."

[13]Sharon Weinhold, ASA (FM&C), private communication, August 1997.

property under a federal agency's control to an outside entity. Expansion in the use of in-kind payments to support activities on the installation other than those related to the lease would allow the commanders the flexibility to use the money where it will better serve the entire installation. Eliminating the requirement that all receipts be reapportioned, thus delaying their use for a year, will ensure that rent receipts are available immediately for use at the installation. The installation could deposit the receipts in a depository account. These changes, if enacted, should greatly increase a commander's flexibility and provide an incentive to expand the use of PPP leases to exploit their full potential to generate additional revenue.

ACTIONS BY ORGANIZATIONS WITHIN THE DEPARTMENT OF DEFENSE

The legislative changes summarized above have facilitated the use of PPPs. Recent actions by various organizations within the Department of Defense have also contributed to producing a climate more conducive to the use of PPPs. As a result, some DoD organizations are now considering PPPs for the first time. Below we present a synopsis of the key features of some major high-level government reviews and studies.

None of these actions alone explicitly directs the military use of PPPs in the future. Collectively, however, the rhetoric of the reviews and studies portrays a PPP-friendly environment, one that encourages entrepreneurial approaches and the use of more commercial business practices and partnering. In this light, one can view PPPs as an integral part of this new pro-business-like climate within the DoD.

Quadrennial Defense Review

The Quadrennial Defense Review (QDR) emphasized the need to reengineer the DoD's infrastructure and business practices through a "Revolution in Business Affairs." This new Revolution in Business Affairs (RBA) parallels the now-familiar Revolution in Military Affairs, whose goal is to harness advanced technologies, concepts, doctrine, and organizations so as to transform today's combat forces into future forces with revolutionary military capabilities.

In essence, the RBA has a companion role in the support and infrastructure area. It is broader than simply implementing current acquisition reform proposals (e.g., eliminating standards/ specifications or using integrated process/product development team approaches). By emphasizing new business practices, the RBA has the goal of harnessing commercial business practices and commercial processes/products to increase the efficiency and cost-effectiveness of the U.S. military support infrastructure. Specific elements of the RBA include leveraging commercial technology, dual-use technology, and open systems; reducing overhead and streamlining infrastructure; and outsourcing and privatizing a wide range of support activities.[14]

Many of the tenets of the RBA are consistent with the objectives of PPPs. For example, PPPs can be used to effectively leverage commercial technologies through research collaborations with industry. Also, PPPs can be used to make infrastructure more efficient and cost-effective through collaborative arrangements with commercial developers, operators, and managers.

National Defense Panel

The National Defense Panel (NDP) has been tasked to assess the Quadrennial Defense Review and provide alternatives to it. As part of this analysis, the NDP has isolated a list of fourteen special issues that need to be integrated with its development of QDR alternatives. Two of the special issues are "infrastructure" and "science and technology."[15]

Although the scope of the white papers being prepared for each special issue is still being defined, in the case of the science and technology issue, there is a major emphasis on maintaining technological superiority.[16] The notion of exploiting the efficiency and cost-effectiveness of the commercial sector is a key element of this issue. PPPs provide a good means to do this.

---

[14] *Report of the Quadrennial Defense Review,* May 1997, p. 15.

[15] "NDP Sees 14 'Special Issues' in Developing QDR Alternatives," *Inside the Army,* July 12, 1997, p. 9.

[16] Emile Ettedgui, private communication, August 1997.

Plan for Consolidation of Defense Labs and T&E Centers

As part of the FY96 National Defense Authorization Act, Congress has directed additional DoD efforts to improve its science and technology activities. Section 177 of the act requires the development of a five-year plan for the consolidation and restructuring of defense laboratories and test and evaluation (T&E) centers. A principal requirement of this authorization is that costs of the laboratory and T&E infrastructure are to be reduced by at least 20 percent by FY05.[17]

A variety of cost-reduction measures have been suggested to achieve this stringent goal. Three generic approaches are proposed: reduction, restructuring, and revitalization. Revitalization includes cross-service sharing, improving efficiencies, and reducing costs of operations and maintenance.[18] One can read into this a broad enough charter to include PPPs as effective mechanisms to save or offset costs through cost-sharing R&D collaborations and revenue-generating infrastructure developments.

Defense Science Board Studies

Recent Defense Science Board (DSB) studies[19] have also made recommendations consistent with using PPPs. The application of commercial practices is the key. A commercial-style research and development model has been proposed. This model features "flexible performance" contracting using the Other Transactions contractual instrument. A principal tenet of this commercial model is public trust—without cost-based contracting and government oversight. This tenet is consistent with the characteristics that define PPPs.

---

[17] Memorandum from the Deputy Secretary of Defense, "Plan for Consolidation of Defense Laboratories and Test and Evaluation (T&E) Centers," May 1, 1996.

[18] Report to Congress, *Vision 21: The Plan for 21st Century Laboratories and Test and Evaluation Centers of the Department of Defense*, April 30, 1996.

[19] *Report of the Defense Science Board 1996 Summer Study on Achieving an Innovative Support Structure for 21st Century Military Superiority: Higher Performance at Lower Costs*, Washington, D.C.: Defense Science Board, November 1996. *Report of the Defense Science Board Task Force on Defense Acquisition Reform (Phase III): A Streamlined Approach to Weapons Systems Research, Development and Acquisition: The Application of Commercial Practices*, Washington, D.C.: Defense Science Board, May 1996.

While these DSB studies do not state explicitly that PPPs should be used (except for one reference to Other Transactions), they do discuss a new commercial-like environment—one in which PPPs can flourish. The studies expound the need for efficiencies, initiatives, and innovations—all the things that PPPs inherently encourage.

Actions by Specific Commands and Agencies

Specific commands and agencies have taken actions that support the DoD's application and extended use of PPPs. A sample of these activities includes the following:

a. The Defense Contract Management Command (DCMC), anticipating a growth in the use of agreements issued under the 10 USC 2371 Other Transactions authority, has developed expertise in the Post Award Authority (PAA) of administering PPP contractual instruments. This is a new service that the DCMC provides to the military services (as well as DARPA). To facilitate the provision of this new service, DCMC will also provide limited assistance with preaward negotiations. Four regional offices have been designated to administer PAA of Other Transactions and Cooperative Agreements.

b. Several AMC subordinate commands have taken the initiative to set up internal mechanisms to explore PPP opportunities. For example, Soldiers Systems Command has formed a process action team (PAT) to investigate PPP possibilities at Natick.

c. Within the Department of the Army, a proposal has been generated to set up an asset management team to identify opportunities for the Army to use its infrastructure assets to obtain revenue and in-kind returns from collaborative projects with the private sector. As a first step in implementing this proposal, the Assistant Chief of Staff for Installation Management has been tasked to study existing leases and excess space.

ACTIVITIES AT THE LOCAL GOVERNMENT LEVEL

At the local/state government level, there is a groundswell of PPP activities involving developers. More and more public agencies, universities, and school districts are teaming up with developers to plan, finance, and develop a range of projects—from office buildings, hotels, and entertainment/retail centers to convention centers, correctional facilities, sports facilities, and housing.

A primary attraction of public/private development partnerships is that they can be mutually beneficial to all parties. While public entities can provide incentives, private developers add essential ingredients such as knowledge and insight on markets, entrepreneurial orientation, vision and creativity, development and management skills, prospective tenants or buyers, and risk capital.[20]

The annual volume of construction of new public/private developments will reach $22 billion this year. This volume is expected to expand to $25 to $30 billion next year.[21] This continued growth at the local level will spur other government agencies, such as the Army, to engage in more PPPs in the future.

Growth in the market is anticipated for several reasons:[22]

a. Both private investors and developers and government entities have become comfortable with the process of forming PPPs and have become confident that such partnerships can meet their performance expectations.

b. Private developers and public officials recognize that PPPs, compared with traditional project financing, are more flexible and allow for greater creativity in project financing, development, and management.

c. Many public entities lack the resources and real estate expertise to complete major public projects. These entities believe that the risks of developing resources alone far outweigh the rewards.

The first two reasons are applicable to the Army as well as local governments.

---

[20]John Stainback, "Advantages of Public/Private Development Partnerships," *Urban Land*, July 1997, pp. 24–27 and 60–64.
[21]Ibid.
[22]Ibid.

SETTING THE TREND

As we have discussed in previous chapters, PPPs are not entirely new to the Army. As shown in Table 3.1, most of the Army's PPP activity has been in the infrastructure arena. In FY95, the Army generated an estimated $69 million (FY95$) from infrastructure PPPs. During the same period, the Army only generated an estimated $300,000 (FY95$) from intellectual property PPPs. By FY95, laws permitting both infrastructure and intellectual property PPPs had been in effect for more than a decade. But as the numbers in Table 3.1 indicate, the Army has clearly benefited more from infrastructure PPPs than from intellectual property PPPs and has not yet begun to explore financial arrangement PPPs.

Infrastructure PPPs

One reason that there are more infrastructure PPPs might be that the "product or potential product" is known. The infrastructure "product" (e.g., the land being leased, the building being modernized, the equipment being shared) physically exists or can be created without the parties wondering "what it will look like." Its characteristics are known to the Army and its partners. In an infrastructure PPP, the parties often are not creating a totally new product and designing a collaborative effort around it. Instead, the partners have to negotiate how best to use a known entity for mutual benefit. Since the parties can comfortably describe the uses of the asset, their main task is to negotiate what is acceptable and what is not.

The unknown in infrastructure PPPs is the market demand for the collaborative entity. The uncertainty in market demand will affect the predictability of profits. Despite the uncertainty, however, there is usually enough data for both partners to estimate demand and benefits (including profitability). The estimation is facilitated by the fact that the time horizon for return of benefits to both the Army and its partners is known.

Table 3.1
Estimated Revenues Generated from Army PPPs in FY95

Activity	Estimated FY95 Earnings (FY95$)
Infrastructure	
Agricultural and grazing leasing	$4M
Fish and wildlife conservation	$2M
Production and sale of forest products	$10M
Sale/outlease of excess real/personal property	$18M
Legacy Resource Management Program	$8M
Energy Conservation Investment Program	$11M
Recycling	$10M
Use of Test and Evaluation installations by commercial entities	$6M
Total from infrastructure	$69M
Intellectual property	
Patent and royalty income	$0.3M
Total from intellectual property	$0.3M
Financial arrangement	
Total from financial arrangement	$0.0M

SOURCE: *Source of Funds for Army Use (Other Than Typical Army Appropriations)*, Office of the Assistant Secretary of the Army for Financial Management, Resource Analysis and Business Practices, SAFM-RB (July 1995).

The Navy's PPP with Mazda Corporation illustrates these concepts. Since 1986, the Navy has leased underutilized land at its Port Hueneme Naval Base to Mazda through a PPP that has brought the base up to $1.2 million per year in infrastructure improvements. In return, Mazda has the use of a fenced facility where it can drive the vehicles it offloads on the commercial side of the Port Hueneme shipyard. The leased land also serves as a strategically located Southern California distribution center for Mazda vehicles. In this case, the collaborative entity is the underutilized land being leased to Mazda Corporation. The characteristics of the land (e.g., its size and location) are known to both partners. The Navy's benefit is approximately $1.2 million per year. Mazda's benefit is a conveniently located storage facility that serves its Southern California distribution area. The only unknown is the market demand for Mazda vehicles in the distribution area served by the leased facility. However, it is probably safe to assume that Mazda Corporation has evaluated the "profitability" of leasing the site and has determined that it stands to benefit from the PPP.

Similarly, the government has had a longstanding PPP with the major U.S. airline companies, whereby the government pays a specified fee to the airlines for the privilege of using the airlines' services and equipment to transport military personnel in times of need.[23] In this PPP, the assets are the airline companies' equipment and services. The benefit to the airline companies is the specified fee. The benefit to the government is use of the equipment and services when they are needed. The unknowns in this case are when and in what quantities the government will need the equipment and services. The unknown cannot be predicted, but its acceptance may be eased by the national-security nature of the need.

The government appears to be comfortable with the known and unknown factors in infrastructure PPPs. As indicated by the Navy's discussions with the Norfolk Port Authority on joint endeavors on the Naval Base Norfolk, the military's pursuit of infrastructure PPPs will probably continue and become more innovative.[24] With each new PPP, the government is gaining more PPP experience that might contribute to making the next one easier to devise and accept, thus establishing the PPP approach as a standard method of managing infrastructure.

Intellectual Property PPPs

The Army has only limited experience with intellectual property PPPs. In this class of PPPs, both the product and the market may be unknown to all parties. The product might only be a visualization and the market demand only a prediction based on sketchy information. These unknowns and uncertainties make designing intellectual

---

[23]Civil Reserve Air Fleet Program.

[24]Katherine McIntire Peters, "Funding the Fleet," *Government Executive*, January 1997, pp. 42–45.

property PPPs more difficult, and these difficulties may be slowing the Army's progress toward using them.

In an intellectual property PPP, there may be no physical entity associated with the research effort. Moreover, not only might the product be unknown, the product itself and market demand for it may depend on the outcome of research. The outcome of the research in itself is uncertain because much of the "success" of the research may depend on a timely synergistic combination of innovation by scientists and foresight by management—both intellectual processes whose timely synergism cannot be guaranteed. In addition, the time horizon for return of benefits is likely to be longer in an intellectual property PPP because research usually has to be completed before product development, commercial manufacturing, and marketing can even be planned. These steps may take many years, so there may be an extended period during which both the government and its partners realize limited benefits or none at all.

Hence, intellectual property PPPs have more unknowns and uncertainty, and these factors make them more difficult and time-consuming to conceive, initiate, and carry out. However, as some of our examples indicate, the Army is beginning to explore intellectual property PPPs. As the Army gains more experience with them, it will eventually gain an understanding of their role in helping the Army accomplish its military mission.

Financial Arrangement PPPs

As we begin the discussion of financial arrangement PPPs, it is important to state that Army financial arrangement PPPs will have to meet a stated critical mission need. These PPPs have to be viewed in the context of whether they will help the Army prepare and maintain a level of superiority when faced with combat. Financial arrangement PPPs for the sole purpose of generating revenue will undoubtedly face severe scrutiny and objection. But using innovative financial means to generate revenue for critical Army mission endeavors should fare better. Financial arrangement PPPs need to be discussed in conjunction with specific needs. These needs may manifest themselves in the form of infrastructure or intellectual property elements. As such, not only can product and market unknowns make these arrangements difficult to design for these financial arrangement

PPPs, they are further complicated by a complex layer of financing that must be integrated into the agreement. The Army has limited, if any, experience in structuring such deals. In addition, the Army does not have a formal policy to seek PPP financing for its endeavors. These two factors may explain why the Army has yet to explore this area.

The Army can begin to explore financial arrangement PPPs by observing some existing programs. For example, some foreign governments, state governments, and municipalities have worked alongside financial institutions and developers to explore innovative means of financing large-scale infrastructure projects.

A Price Waterhouse study in 1990 highlighted such innovation in financing.[25] One project it describes is the Chicago–Kansas City Tollway, which was financed using a three-layer financing arrangement. The first layer, involving serial zero-coupon senior lien debt, was the most secure and made up 75 percent of the project's capital. The second layer, made up of mezzanine financing, was at greater risk and was 18 percent of the project's capital. The third layer, involving common equity, was the highest-risk grouping of funds and made up 7 percent of the project's capital.

Similarly, in the Far East, the Eastern Harbor Crossing Development (rail and motor vehicle tunnel connecting Quarry Bay on Hong Kong Island to Cha Kwo Ling, Kowloon on the mainland of the People's Republic of China) was prohibited from receiving any public funds. The development was financed by integrating equity contributions with a debt package that consisted of revolving loans and installment sale facilities.

The Army can also look to private-sector corporations to learn about financial arrangements and how they can be used to accomplish specific objectives. For instance, General Electric may issue a bond for the purpose of using the proceeds to construct a manufacturing plant. Another example would be Sony establishing an endowed professorship in an academic department of its choosing. Corporations often enter into financial arrangements to accomplish a set

---

[25]Price Waterhouse, *Public-Private Partnership in Infrastructure: A Primer*, Washington, D.C.: Price Waterhouse, Transportation and Utilities Finance Group, 1990.

objective. The Army, through financial arrangement PPPs, can do the same to accomplish objectives relevant to its military mission. This notion will be discussed further in the next chapter.

Chapter Four

A PROJECTED EVALUATION OF PUBLIC-PRIVATE PARTNERSHIPS

Extrapolating on the trends described in Chapter Three, there is likely to be more use of PPPs in the future. In this chapter we look at what the evolving use of PPPs might include. We have compiled a list of thirty-six candidate PPP concepts.[1] The concepts are novel ideas, many of which have not yet been tried by the Army or any other military service. A few of the ideas are extensions of existing programs in the military and other institutions. Other ideas are more radical concepts that have no precedents or relationship to any government program. Some ideas are innovative combinations of practices that have occurred in different fields. While we have presented the entire scope of ideas, not all are appropriate for the Army to include in its general repertoire. Indeed, not all of these ideas may yet be legal for the Army to undertake. The list is intended to show the broad range of PPPs in the infrastructure, intellectual property, and financial arrangement areas that may evolve in the future and stimulate thought about them. The list should not be interpreted as a prescription for immediate action.

There are several ways that the Army can choose ideas to pursue. One is to determine the feasibility of the ideas and then pursue all those that are feasible. Another way is to determine feasibility and then screen the feasible subset with respect to the benefits that each idea is likely to bring to the Army. Ideas that are feasible and that

---

[1]Detailed descriptions of the specific PPP ideas are given in Appendix A. These candidates resulted from looking at what's going on in academia, the financial world, and the commercial sector. The list is not intended to be comprehensive, only representative of the spectrum of PPP possibilities.

appear most promising with respect to their potential benefits can then be proactively pursued by the Army.

As shown in Figure 4.1, a third approach is to perform feasibility and benefits evaluations and then combine the results to categorize the ideas into subsets. In this scheme, the Army can set its own objective and select ideas accordingly. For example, one choice for the objective of the categorization could be to choose ideas from infrastructure, intellectual property, and financial arrangements so that the subset contains ideas from all three areas. In addition, the subset could contain ideas that are feasible and ideas that are not yet legal, acceptable, or attractive. Also, the subset can contain ideas that offer a range of benefits. The subset can then form the basis of a strategic approach for the Army. By pursuing a subset of ideas with a variety of ranges, the Army will not be venturing into ideas that are all marginal in terms of feasibility, but can concentrate on implementing a few that are legal, acceptable, and attractive, while pursuing legislation on an exceptionally promising idea that is not yet legal.

For the one or two ideas in the subset that are not yet particularly attractive, the Army can focus on variants that make them more attractive. Some ideas may be better pursued using a pilot program, but starting one or two at a time is a more prudent approach than starting a dozen. By pursuing ideas that offer a range of benefits, the Army stands to gain in all areas rather than "putting all its eggs in one

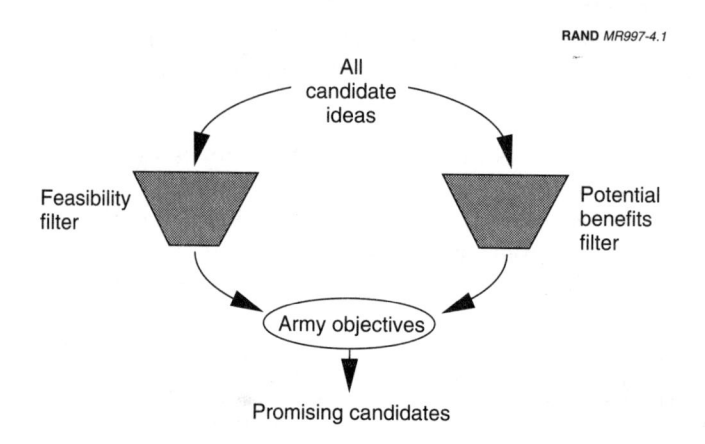

Figure 4.1—Screening Tool for Identifying Promising Candidates

basket." This subset approach offers the Army a chance to experiment with ideas that appear more revolutionary, but that may also hold more potential for returns. At the same time, by also pursuing ideas that have some precedents, the Army stands to reap some benefits from its gradual expansion into PPPs.

In this chapter we present a screening tool for evaluating feasibility and a screening tool for evaluating potential benefits. Both tools are intended to yield first-order indications of feasibility and potential benefits based on common sense and reason. The Army can use these tools to winnow lists of ideas down to ones that it might want to look into in more detail. More in-depth study would be required to determine the actual promise of each concept.

FEASIBILITY CRITERIA

When considering whether one specific idea can be successfully implemented, many factors have to be considered. Among these factors is the idea's feasibility in terms of its legality; whether it will be acceptable publicly, politically, and within the Army; and its attractiveness to potential private partners.

In this section we discuss these three feasibility criteria. An idea must meet all three criteria for it to be feasible: the idea must be legal; it must be acceptable; and it must be attractive enough to draw commercial firms into collaboration with the Army. Ideas that meet all three feasibility criteria are more likely to be successfully implemented by the Army. Ideas that at present meet only one or two of the criteria can still be worth pursuing, but the Army may have to take actions to make them legal, acceptable, and attractive to private firms.

Legality

As discussed in Chapter Three, recent legislative changes indicate a trend toward establishing an environment that is more conducive to PPPs. Of course, the legality of each specific idea must still be determined. Most of the ideas presented below are new to the Army, and in some cases the legality of implementing them may be fuzzy. A specific idea may have no precedent with respect to the intent of applicable laws and the Army implementation. In such cases, it may be helpful to look at similar ideas that may already be implemented in other services, DoD agencies such as DARPA, other federal agencies, local governments, or in the commercial world.

When the legality of a specific idea is in question, the Army needs to resolve the issue by establishing its status under current laws, seeking legislative changes that will allow the Army to implement the idea, or rejecting the idea. The Army's course of action will be governed by a variety of factors, including the merits of the idea, how the Army expects to benefit, and the effort involved in establishing its legality.

Of the three courses of action, the most ambitious is seeking changes to current laws to make implementation of the idea legal. Although this course of action may involve considerable effort, in some cases the merit of the specific idea justifies its pursuit.

For example, in 1985 the Army decided to move the 10th Mountain Division to Fort Drum, New York. Before this announcement, Fort Drum was a tertiary installation with few facilities. Infrastructure shortcomings, including family housing, meant the Army would have to accelerate the budgetary, procurement, and building processes to accomplish its goal of expeditiously moving the 10th Mountain Division. The Army Chief of Staff identified family housing as the "pacing factor" for the buildup of the division. To expeditiously transfer the division and circumvent the arduous budget/procurement process, the Army pursued and obtained legislative authority (Public Law 99-145, sections 801–803) to establish PPPs with real estate developers to quickly build family housing. The PPPs resulted in the developers building 2,000 housing units to Army specifications on developer-chosen sites in exchange for a twenty-year Army lease. As part of the PPPs, the Army guarantees 97 percent occupancy and pays $550 per month for shelter rent and $150 per month for maintenance. Routine administrative actions such as assignments and terminations are handled by the Army Family Housing Office. At the end of the twenty-year leases, the Army can buy out the developers, negotiate new leases, or walk away. The pursuit of legislation to permit PPPs resulted in family housing units being built in record time, and the Army met its goal of expeditiously transferring the 10th Mountain Division.

Acceptance

Even when an idea's legality has been established, successful implementation requires that it also be acceptable. That is, legality does not always indicate that the public will consider it proper for the Army to pursue certain PPP ideas. For example, the general public may think that it is improper for the Army to pursue ideas that generate revenue per se.[2]

Similarly, some ideas may not be well received by the political community. For example, joint ownership of facilities may be sufficiently radical that the uncertainty of its implications may make such an idea infeasible.[3]

The Army, itself, may find some ideas unacceptable even though they are legal. The Army has been conducting its business according to well-established processes and procedures for a long time. Thus, an idea may prove unacceptable within the Army simply because the Army is used to doing business in a certain fashion and the new idea may seem contrary to processes, procedures, values, or precedence. For example, some in the Army may be uncomfortable with the concept of joint employees.[4]

Attractiveness to Private Firms

A PPP requires one or more private partners. Hence, the ideas presented in this chapter can be successful only if the idea is attractive to private firms. Ideas that are likely to be attractive are those in which the private party stands to profit or otherwise benefit from the PPP. Different firms will have different thresholds that define whether or not they are interested in an idea, so the Army must remain flexible in this regard.

The more firms that inquire about collaborating with the Army, the more likely it is that the Army will be able to fashion an agreement

---

[2] See Chapter One for a discussion of revenue generation.

[3] See Appendix A, "Infrastructure" subsection, for a discussion of joint ownership of facilities.

[4] See Appendix A, "Infrastructure" subsection, for a discussion of joint employees.

with one of them. To broaden the field of candidates, the Army can advertise and inform commercial firms about its willingness to negotiate certain types of PPPs, but the concept itself must be appealing for the advertising to be effective. Hence, even if an idea is legal and acceptable, successful implementation requires that it be appealing enough to draw candidate partners into pursuing a PPP with the Army.

EVALUATION OF SPECIFIC IDEAS

Below we present the specific PPP ideas according to area: infrastructure, intellectual property, and financial arrangements. Within the three areas, the ideas are evaluated with respect to feasibility and benefits.

Infrastructure

Table 4.1 shows six infrastructure ideas evaluated with respect to the three aspects of feasibility: legality, acceptance, and attractiveness. The ideas, described in Appendix A, have a wide range of feasibility. For example, leasing out facilities and assets that have excess capacity is likely to be legal, acceptable to all parties, and attractive enough to attract potential private partners. On the other hand, acceptance is questionable for co-use of laboratories/R&D assets. The feasibility of joint ownership of noncritical facilities and assets is also questionable, but the Army is likely to find that charging a fee for use of its services, facilities, or equipment is an implementable idea. The feasibility of the other PPP infrastructure ideas is indicated in the table.

Table 4.2 shows the infrastructure ideas evaluated with respect to the potential benefits each might bring to the Army. In general, the ideas are most likely to generate revenues or present opportunities for the Army to leverage its resources, reduce costs, or decrease outlays. For example, leasing facilities or assets with excess capacity and offering tours are likely to generate revenues. Using joint employees is likely to offer opportunities for leveraging assets, reducing costs, or decreasing outlays. A few of the ideas also offer the possibility of improving the Army's readiness posture by keeping infrastructure items within Army control. For example, the use of joint employees could

Table 4.1

Feasibility of PPP Ideas in Infrastructure

	Legality	Acceptance			Attractiveness
		Public	Political	Within Army	
Lease out facilities/assets	Likely	Likely	Likely	Likely	Likely
Fee for use of services, facilities, or equipment	Likely	Likely	Likely	Likely	Likely
Joint ownership of noncritical facilities and assets	Doubtful	Possible	Doubtful	Doubtful	Possible
Joint employees	Possible	Possible	Doubtful	Doubtful	Doubtful
Timeshare equipment/facilities	Possible	Possible	Doubtful	Doubtful	Possible
Co-use of laboratories / R&D assets	Doubtful	Possible	Doubtful	Doubtful	Possible

offer this benefit because the joint employees could quickly revert to being full-time Army employees in times of national need without the Army having to go through the hiring process. Leasing out facilities/assets could also bring this benefit by allowing the Army to quickly return facilities and equipment to Army use in times of need.

Intellectual Property

Table 4.3 shows eight intellectual property concepts evaluated with respect to the three aspects of feasibility. Again, some concepts are likely to be legal, acceptable, and attractive, and some are questionable in terms of all three aspects. Army efforts toward becoming a third party to established R&D programs such as DARPA projects and SBIR efforts are likely to be feasible and welcome because the Army will bring in some outside money and a new viewpoint to the programs that could benefit the other federal agency and the private partners. Other Transactions joint ventures and equity funds appear to be legal, but the concepts may be sufficiently radical that acceptance and attracting private partners may be the main obstacles to implementation. A few ideas, such as design for retrofit and design with lower-cost substitutes, may not expressly require a PPP, but a PPP would greatly enhance the success of such ideas because both would require the Army to work very closely with its private partner at an early stage of product development, and this mutual trust would contribute to successful product development.

Table 4.4 shows the intellectual property ideas evaluated with respect to the potential benefits each might bring to the Army. Most of the ideas are likely to produce opportunities for the Army to leverage assets, reduce costs, or decrease outlays. A few ideas, such as the Other Transactions joint venture, equity fund, and incubator arrangements, also offer the possibility of creating new assets and generating some revenue. Leasing technology with the option to buy is most likely to reduce costs or decrease outlays, but this idea could also improve the Army's readiness posture through more frequent or quicker upgrading of equipment. The consolidated research fund and incubator arrangement are likely to facilitate early influence on technology. A more promising way of reducing costs might be to design equipment with retrofitting in mind or design equipment that uses lower-cost substitutes.

Table 4.2
Potential Benefits of PPP Ideas for Infrastructure

	Leverage Assets, Reduce Costs	Increase Value of Assets	Create New Capabilities or Assets	Influence Technology Early	Improve Readiness Posture	Generate Revenue
Lease out facilities/assets	Doubtful	Doubtful	Doubtful	Doubtful	Possible	Likely
Fee for use of services, facilities, or equipment	Doubtful	Doubtful	Doubtful	Doubtful	Possible	Likely
Joint ownership of noncritical facilities or assets	Likely	Possible	Doubtful	Doubtful	Doubtful	Doubtful
Joint employees	Likely	Doubtful	Doubtful	Possible	Possible	Doubtful
Timeshare equipment/facilities	Likely	Possible	Doubtful	Doubtful	Possible	Doubtful
Co-use of laboratories/ R&D assets	Likely	Doubtful	Doubtful	Doubtful	Doubtful	Doubtful

Table 4.3
Feasibility of PPP Ideas in Intellectual Property

	Legality	Acceptance			Attractiveness
		Public	Political	Within Army	
Third party with established programs	Likely	Likely	Likely	Likely	Likely
Design for retrofit	Likely	Likely	Likely	Likely	Likely
Design with lower-cost substitutes	Likely	Possible	Possible	Possible	Possible
Other transaction joint venture	Likely	Possible	Possible	Possible	Possible
Equity fund	Likely	Possible	Possible	Possible	Possible
Lease technology with option to buy	Likely	Likely	Possible	Possible	Likely
Consolidated research fund	Likely	Likely	Likely	Likely	Possible
Incubator arrangement	Likely	Likely	Possible	Likely	Likely

Table 4.4
Potential Benefits of PPP Ideas for Intellectual Property

	Leverage Assets, Reduce Costs	Increase Value of Assets	Create New Capabilities or Assets	Influence Technology Early	Improve Readiness Posture	Generate Revenue
Third party with established program	Likely	Doubtful	Doubtful	Likely	Doubtful	Doubtful
Design for retrofit	Likely	Doubtful	Doubtful	Likely	Doubtful	Doubtful
Design with lower cost substitutes	Likely	Doubtful	Doubtful	Doubtful	Doubtful	Likely
Other Transaction joint venture	Likely	Doubtful	Possible	Doubtful	Doubtful	Possible
Equity fund	Likely	Doubtful	Possible	Doubtful	Doubtful	Possible
Lease technology with option to buy	Likely	Doubtful	Doubtful	Doubtful	Possible	Doubtful
Consolidated research fund	Likely	Doubtful	Doubtful	Likely	Doubtful	Doubtful
Incubator arrangement	Possible	Possible	Possible	Likely	Doubtful	Possible

Financial Arrangements

As stated in the previous chapter, financial arrangement PPPs have to be discussed in conjunction with specific military needs. These specific needs may manifest themselves in the form of elements related to infrastructure or intellectual property assets.

For the Army, financial arrangement PPPs are probably the least understood and potentially the most controversial, yet they may open untold opportunities. However, as we have mentioned, there is virtually no Army activity in this area. Hence, our list of specific ideas in this area is both longer and perhaps more unconventional than the infrastructure and intellectual property ideas shown above.

Table 4.5 shows the financial arrangement ideas evaluated with respect to the three aspects of feasibility. Although this set of ideas may appear to be the most radical, some of the ideas do have precedents, and the Army may feel most comfortable implementing those ideas first. For instance, negotiating discounts might be legal and acceptable. It is also quite possible for this idea to be attractive to private firms in exchange for some benefit such as a high volume of Army business or continuing Army patronage over a period of time. The Navy is already trying out this idea in its Energy Vision program at Naval Base Norfolk. Under this program the Navy evaluated its energy needs and established a course to meet those needs at the lowest cost. One aspect of Energy Vision is to have a broker negotiate discounted energy prices for the Navy.[5]

Another feasible idea is for the Army to dispose of unneeded equipment through auctions rather than giving away the surplus, as it often does now. Establishing an alumni fund and negotiating exchange privileges are also ideas that are not likely to generate significant opposition. Some ideas such as nontraditional cost sharing may be feasible or highly contested, depending on the exact application. An Army information-broker service, in which the Army charges fees for sale or use of its patents, test data, or other data bases, could be a feasible extension of the infrastructure idea of leasing out excess-capacity facilities or property.

---

[5]Current DoD regulations are barring implementation of this aspect of the program.

Table 4.5
Feasibility of PPP Ideas in Financial Arrangements

		Acceptance			
	Legality	Public	Political	Within Army	Attractiveness
Negotiate discounts	Possible	Likely	Likely	Likely	Possible
Negotiate exchange privileges	Likely	Likely	Likely	Likely	Possible
Nontraditional cost sharing*	Possible	Possible	Possible	Possible	Possible
Auctions to dispose of unneeded equipment	Likely	Likely	Likely	Likely	Likely
Army affinity credit card	Possible	Possible	Possible	Possible	Possible
Purchasing rights	Possible	Possible	Possible	Possible	Possible
Project finance	Doubtful	Possible	Doubtful	Doubtful	Possible
Army information broker fund	Possible	Possible	Possible	Possible	Possible
Army loan program	Doubtful	Possible	Doubtful	Doubtful	Possible
Army real estate investment trust	Doubtful	Possible	Doubtful	Doubtful	Possible

*Feasibility will depend on exact implementation.

The financial arrangements list also contains more radical ideas, which might not be feasible now but might, over time, be made feasible. The most revolutionary notions, such as real estate investment trusts, would require considerable effort to even formulate, much less implement. It should be understood, however, that "radical" ideas do not develop solely from bold initiatives. The complexity of the financial system fosters evolution of instruments such as bonds and warrants to high levels of sophistication to meet real needs. What looks bold at any one time tends to look ordinary a few years later.

Table 4.6 shows the financial arrangement ideas evaluated with respect to the potential benefits each might bring to the Army. As might be expected, most of the financial arrangement ideas offer the Army opportunities to generate revenue or to leverage assets, reduce costs, or decrease outlays. For example, negotiating discounts is likely to leverage Army assets, reduce costs, or decrease outlays. On the other hand, an Army affinity card is likely to generate revenue and could reduce some costs, depending on how the revenue is used. Some of the other ideas also have the potential to generate revenue.

Table 4.6
Potential Benefits of PPP Ideas for Financial Arrangements

	Leverage Assets, Reduce Costs, or Decrease Outlays	Increase Value of Assets	Create New Capabilities or Assets	Influence Technology Early	Improve Readiness Posture	Generate Revenue
Negotiate discounts	Likely	Doubtful	Doubtful	Doubtful	Doubtful	Doubtful
Negotiate exchange privileges	Likely	Possible	Doubtful	Doubtful	Doubtful	Doubtful
Nontraditional cost sharing*	Possible	Doubtful	Doubtful	Doubtful	Doubtful	Possible
Auctions to dispose of unneeded equipment	Possible	Doubtful	Doubtful	Doubtful	Doubtful	Likely
Affinity credit card	Possible	Doubtful	Doubtful	Doubtful	Doubtful	Likely
Purchasing rights	Possible	Doubtful	Doubtful	Doubtful	Doubtful	Doubtful
Project Finance	Possible	Doubtful	Doubtful	Doubtful	Doubtful	Likely
Army information broker fund	Possible	Doubtful	Doubtful	Doubtful	Doubtful	Likely
Army loan program	Possible	Doubtful	Doubtful	Doubtful	Doubtful	Likely
Army real estate investment trust	Possible	Doubtful	Doubtful	Doubtful	Doubtful	Likely

*Benefits depend on the specific nontraditional cost-share arrangement (equity, warrants, future discounting, etc.).

Chapter Five
CLOSING REMARKS AND RECOMMENDATIONS

In this report we have defined PPPs to be collaborative agreements that are fashioned for mutual benefit. PPPs can offer the Army a variety of benefits, including opportunities to leverage resources; reduce costs, capital investments, and outlays; and increase the value of its assets, create new capabilities and assets, influence technology developments, improve its readiness posture, and generate revenue. Our research shows that most Army PPPs have been in the infrastructure area, but the Army is beginning to experiment with intellectual property PPPs. The Army has not yet fully explored financial arrangement PPPs. We have identified access to capital, marketing expertise, operating expertise, and access to leading-edge technology as the primary private-sector contributions that best complement the Army's infrastructure asset and intellectual property holdings. The Army should look toward the private sector for these same contributions when it begins to explore financial arrangement PPPs.

Our study of legislation over several decades indicates a distinct trend toward creating an environment that is more conducive to PPPs. In addition, recent actions by federal agencies and local governments all point toward more PPPs in the future. These trends should further motivate the Army to enter into more PPPs and explore more novel PPPs. As such, we presented a range of innovative PPPs in the infrastructure, intellectual property, and financial arrangement areas and demonstrated tools the Army can use to screen the ideas. To help determine which ideas to pursue, we showed an initial screening of the ideas for feasibility in terms of legality, acceptability, and attractiveness. In addition, we showed the types of benefits each idea was likely to bring. By combining the results of the feasibility and benefits examinations, the Army can develop a strategic approach to its gradual expansion into greater use of PPPs.

Before the Army can consider expanding its participation in PPPs, it must first have a good understanding of which ideas are feasible with respect to the Army's contribution. That is, the Army must determine which of its properties are underutilized, which assets have excess capacity, and what intellectual property it owns. Such an internal accounting would allow the Army to develop the ideas in this report with its specific contribution in mind. The identification of the Army's contribution is an essential first step toward exploring any PPP.

This report strives to discuss a wide range of different types of PPPs. Some PPPs can be implemented in the very near future, while others are more revolutionary in nature. In certain cases, PPPs may cause major structural changes in current organizations. These changes will be resented by individuals whose job status would be affected. In other cases, the implementation of PPPs may require the enactment of special congressional legislative authority when they involve activities not fully covered under current statutes. For example, the Willoughby Housing Development[1] and the ARMS program involved such activities. In the Willoughby case, the Department of the Navy requested and obtained special legislation authorizing the development of the land in partnership with the private developers. In the ARMS case, Congress took the initiative to offer legislation and appropriated approximately $200 million to fund the program. The Army should not be put off just because special legislation may be required. As these examples illustrate, such legislation can be obtained if a good case is made.

Once the Army has identified its candidate contributions, it must proactively look for interested private partners. This is a marketing task that can be carried out by a private marketing firm or, if the asset is at a federal laboratory, handled through the laboratory's Office of Research and Technology Applications (ORTA). For example, the National Aeronautics and Space Administration (NASA) uses the Re-

---

[1] See the discussion of the Willoughby Housing Development in Appendix B.

gional Technology Transfer Center to match its intellectual property with private commercialization opportunities. Venture capitalists can also perform this task.

Although PPPs are mutually beneficial, it could take a considerable amount of time and energy to fashion one that is agreeable in all the aspects that are important to the Army and its private partners. The Defense Contract Management Command (DCMC) maintains four regional offices chiefly to support the postaward administration of OTs, CAs, and other nonprocurement instruments, but it also helps to develop nonprocurement agreements.[2] DCMC services could ease some of the agreement development burden, but the Army would still need to periodically assess whether the benefits it expects to attain are worth the time and energy spent to develop an agreement. As the Thayer Hotel case illustrates, many years can pass between formulation of the initial idea and the signing of a PPP. In the hotel case, the expected benefits appear to be well worth the effort, but this may not always be the case. The Army should expect to make "go/no go" decisions based on its best judgment. These decisions should become more routine as it gains experience with different types of PPPs.

Finally, some AMC personnel have raised the concern that the Office of the Secretary of Defense (OSD) will view PPPs that generate revenue as opportunities to reduce budgets by the amount of revenue generated. This concern has merit, as illustrated by the OSD reduction in the 1998 family housing construction budget. The reduction was sought because a PPP program was to be used to develop housing.[3] Clearly, the legislative trends and actions by government agencies discussed in Chapter Three are aimed to encourage PPPs, while this budget reduction concern does the opposite. Several avenues can be taken to alleviate this concern. One is education. Those making budget decisions have to be made aware of the utility of PPPs and understand how budget decisions affect that utility. In this respect, regulatory guidance may be appropriate. A second method of handling this concern is to fashion revenue-generating PPPs, in which the Army's revenue comes in in-kind payments rather than in

---

[2]See Chapter Three and Appendix B for further discussion of DCMC services.

[3]"Officials Defend Cuts in Housing Construction Funds," *Army Times,* March 3, 1997.

cash. In-kind payments are services or products paid for by the private partner that equal the value of the Army's share of the return. For example, in the Navy's Port Hueneme Naval Base PPP with Mazda Corporation, Mazda repaves roads and mends fencing at the installation instead of paying the Navy cash for its lease.[4]

We recommend that the Army consider the proposed PPP ideas using the screening methods as applicable. Each candidate PPP should be analyzed in depth before any decision to proceed to implement the initiative. An AMC Command Counsel legal review should be performed as part of that assessment. Specifically, infrastructure stakeholders should consider the infrastructure PPP ideas described in Appendix A. RDECs should consider the intellectual property ideas described in Appendix A. Those involved with Army finances should consider the financial arrangement PPP ideas described in Appendix A.

We believe that PPPs can return benefits to the Army that other types of agreements may never afford. We encourage the Army to exploit the range of opportunities offered by PPPs to help meet its military needs. Consistent with this objective, we recommend that the Army put together a road show on PPPs to present to Army middle management personnel. It could be a powerful change agent for the Army. The road show could build on some of the examples shown in this report and draw on other service experiences, PPP examples from educational institutions (which are doing a lot of PPPs and have a lot to say about them), and other public sector/private sector activities. The Army should also compile its growing PPP experiences into a corporate knowledge base that is easily accessible by Army personnel. This data base would not report on lessons learned but would be a resource for those who want examples of what has been done to date so that they can better exercise their entrepreneurial spirits.

---

[4] See Chapter Three for further discussion of the Port Hueneme Naval Base agreement with Mazda Corporation.

Appendix A
SUMMARIES OF SPECIFIC IDEAS

This appendix contains summary descriptions of the specific ideas for PPPs presented in Chapter Four. The ideas are presented according to area: infrastructure, intellectual property, and financial arrangements.

INFRASTRUCTURE

Leasing Out Facilities and Assets

Leasing out facilities such as laboratory space and other assets such as R&D equipment is highly likely to be feasible with respect to legality, acceptance, and attractiveness. This idea would involve a private firm renting laboratory facilities or equipment that is not to be used by the Army during the lease period. The Army simply collects a fee and turns over the leased facility or equipment to the renter, and the renting firm conducts its business without interaction with the Army. Leasing of laboratory space or other R&D assets such as test and evaluation facilities may already be taking place, but probably on a limited scale. Other federal agencies such as the Department of Energy have established procedures for leasing out their facilities, so the Army has examples to study if it chooses to pursue this idea. The leasing of Army facilities to private firms is likely to be an idea acceptable to the Army, to the public, and to politicians. The attractiveness of this idea will ultimately be determined by the specific facility or asset offered for lease, but some commercial firms might find this option attractive because it can give them immediate access to facilities.

Leasing out facilities and other assets is likely to generate revenue from the leasing fees. In addition, leasing could improve the Army's readiness posture because the leased infrastructure items will remain in Army control and can be reverted to Army use in case of national emergency.

Fee for Use of Services and Facilities

Fee for use of services and facilities or equipment is also highly likely to be legal, acceptable, and attractive. In this scheme, the Army can perform the service and charge a fee for its services and use of equipment, or the Army may simply charge the user for the equipment on a per-use basis and let the user operate the equipment. Of course, the Army could only implement this idea where there is some excess capability that selected firms or the general public can use. For example, the Army has a network of videoteleconferencing sites. Not all of those sites are being used at full capacity, so the Army could conceivably offer videoteleconferencing services to firms or the public for a fee-for-use basis when the sites are not being used by the military. Since these sites are operated under an agreement with a communications firm, the agreement with that firm may have to be modified. A three-party PPP where the Army, the communications firm, and the customer all benefit would be the ideal implementation of this example.

Making excess capacity facilities, equipment, and services available to the public on a fee-for-use basis would generate revenue and possibly improve the Army's readiness posture in some cases when revenue can pay for modernization or defray costs.

Joint Ownership of Noncritical Assets

Joint ownership of noncritical assets involves the Army and a private party both owning the infrastructure item. The Army may use the item exclusively and pay its partner a fee, or the private party may use it and pay the Army a fee. When the Army needs the infrastructure item, it can preempt the private party's use. Such a scheme could allow the Army to acquire state-of-the-art facilities or equipment for less outlay from its budget. Alternatively, the Army could sell a share of some noncritical assets or facilities for a one-time gain and let the private party update, maintain, and use the asset until the Army needs it. This arrangement would preserve the asset for Army use during national emergencies.

Joint ownership of noncritical infrastructure items might be a way of leveraging Army assets to reduce costs or decrease outlays. Joint ownership could even increase the value of the jointly owned assets because the private-party joint owner could help pay for improvements and upkeep.

Joint Employees

Joint employees, where an employee works part time for the Army and part time for a private firm, is an idea that requires considerably more investigation. Its legality may be questionable (e.g., conflict of interest issues), and such an idea may be difficult to accept. However, it may be attractive to firms and the Army because joint employees could reduce personnel costs for both parties while retaining the amount and type of expertise that both parties need. For example, joint employees might be a solution in a case where scarce and highly paid expertise is required, but neither the private party nor the Army needs full-time employees with the required skills.

This kind of employee arrangement might also allow the Army to influence technology early if the joint employees facilitate communication between the Army and private-sector scientists. In addition, in time of need, the joint employees could quickly revert to full-time Army status without the Army having to go through the hiring process. (See Chapter Four for a discussion of joint employees.)

Timesharing of Facilities or Equipment

Timesharing of facilities or equipment, where the Army uses the asset during part of each day, week, month, or year and the private party uses it during the other times, might be legal and publicly acceptable as well as an attractive way for both the Army and a private partner to save some money, but such a practice may not be acceptable politically or within the Army.

Timesharing of facilities or equipment could reduce Army costs and outlays. The timeshared infrastructure item might also increase in value because the private party may help pay for improvements and maintenance. Also, in time of national need, the Army could revert the arrangement back to full-time Army use, thus improving the Army's readiness posture.

Co-Use of Army Laboratories/R&D Assets

Co-use of laboratories and other R&D assets means that the Army shares the use of its facilities with a private firm. The private firm pays the Army a fee, and the employees of both the Army and the private firm work side by side, using the same equipment and facilities to perform their tasks. Such a PPP would have to address a host of issues, including working conditions, boundaries on the space and equipment that is to be shared, intellectual property issues that might arise from "shared knowledge" that may occur in such a working environment, and damage and maintenance procedures and costs. The fee the Army charges may be based on actual usage, flat fee, or some other formula. The revenue the Army receives can then be applied to maintaining the facility, paying for the Army projects that are carried out at that site, funding future research projects, or some other designated use.

This idea could be attractive to a private firm because it could gain use of facilities and equipment at lower cost than it would spend to acquire such assets on its own, but the idea may not be legal for the Army to undertake, and its acceptance is questionable in many cases.

INTELLECTUAL PROPERTY

Third Party with Established Programs

Proactive efforts to identify Army research goals that intersect with those of DARPA, SBIR, and other established programs may be an approach that will allow the Army to gain partial funding of some of its research. This concept is likely to be legal, acceptable, and attractive, but the Army will also have to ensure that its pursuits meet the requirements of the established programs. When suitable intersections are found, the Army can exploit the efforts of the other government agency to facilitate its efforts to find a private partner. Since the Army will also expend some efforts and funds on the project, the other government agency and the private partners will also benefit from this approach.

This scheme could help reduce the Army's cost of research in multi-use technologies. The Army may also benefit by influencing the technology early and be able to buy the quantities and versions it needs at lower prices. Lower prices may be possible because the production costs for the Army's buy could be reduced by the larger production volume of commercial versions of the products.

Design Modularly for Retrofit or Cost

Designing modularly with retrofit in mind does not require a PPP, but the process is likely to be more efficient if the Army makes this requirement known early in the R&D process, and a partnering arrangement could facilitate communications about Army expectations and the developing partner's views. Designing with retrofit in mind is likely to be legal and acceptable. Also, the idea may be attractive to many firms, because modularly designed products may also have high commercial demand. By using this practice, the Army can not only reduce the cost of the version it needs, it may also be able to influence the technology early enough to allow for lower-cost upgrading in the future.

Design with Lower-Cost Substitutes, or Design for Cost

Designing with lower-cost substitutes is likely to be legal and publicly and politically acceptable as well as suitable for attracting private partners. However, although this practice can result in a product that costs less for the Army to buy, the idea may be perceived as resulting in an inferior product and hence may face barriers of acceptance with the Army. We have included this idea as a PPP because for it to work and be acceptable to the Army, the Army must work very closely with a private-party developer to ensure that all Army requirements are met and that the resulting product is not inferior in performance or reliability. The Army would have to make its requirements known early in the R&D phase. This early involvement might lead to an additional price decrease due to production costs that are lowered by the higher production volume of commercial versions of a dual-use product.

Other Transactions Joint Venture

An OTJV is an agreement between the Army and a private firm that takes full advantage of the cost sharing and return-on-investment provisions allowed in Other Transactions agreements. Such an OTJV entity might allow both parties to contribute funds and expertise while a separate management unit is created for the OTJV operation. Both parties would monitor the management unit, and Army participation in the research may be negotiated along with terms for Army sharing in future profits, revenues, or equity in any spin-off unit as a passive investor. The Army could also choose to receive a portion of its return in free or discounted products. For example, if an OTJV results in a dual-use product, the Army can choose to receive one free unit for every hundredth unit sold commercially, up to the number that the Army needs.

Using the provisions of 10 USC §2371, OTJVs can be financially managed using a self-sustaining revolving trust account. The Army would be able to receive investment outlays from the trust account and recovery would be deposited into the account for future R&D efforts. This type of PPP could lower the Army's research expenditures as well as create new Army assets and generate a stream of revenue.

To further illustrate the OTJV concept, we present a hypothetical example. Suppose the Army enters into a CRADA with a technological leader in a particular field. This initial CRADA has few commitments and is aimed at conducting some exploratory research. Suppose, further, that some promising avenues are identified as a result of the CRADA. The Army and its partner then transition the CRADA agreement to an OTJV. The OTJV identifies common goals, and commingled funds and in-kind contributions result in a dual-use product. Since the parties now foresee a commercialization potential, they create a spin-off entity that retains all of the intellectual property from the OTJV. The Army retains passive financial interest in the spin-off unit in the form of a 10 percent equity share. An initial public offering of $200 million would gross $20 million for the Army.

Such an OTJV is likely to be legal and would probably be acceptable and attractive. However, this type of concept is new for the Army and may be surprising to private partners who have more traditional views of doing business with the government. One of the obstacles the Army may face in pursuing this idea is educating itself on joint venture approaches and convincing private parties that it not only can enter in such agreements but also welcomes them.

Army Equity Fund

Another new concept is Army investment in an equity fund. Under this concept, the Army invests a small portion of its R&D funds as a cornerstone limited partner in an equity fund chartered to develop Army and dual-use products and services. As a cornerstone limited partner, the Army helps attract other limited partners who provide the majority of the fund's capital. The Army also avoids conflict of interest by being a limited partner. By investing a relatively small amount (say, 10 percent of the fund's capital), the Army's return is multiplied by the amount provided by the other parties to fund the development of products the Army needs. In addition, the Army may buy dual-use products at a lower cost because production costs are lowered by the usually much larger commercial production. Army returns on its investment in the fund can be deposited in a revolving account and used to research and develop other products of Army interest or reinvest in further R&D equity funds.

To further illustrate this concept, we compare this Army equity fund concept to that of a typical private equity fund. In a typical private equity fund, the general partners have expertise in an industry area and in investment banking. In the Army equity fund, the Army has some expertise in the industry area but very little, if any, in investment banking. The private fund general partners develop a highly focused investment strategy and return-on-investment objectives. Diversification, expressed in terms of limits on single investments (say, 10 percent), is used to minimize risks. The general partners provide the initial capital, which is usually 2.5 to 10 percent of the total. They raise the balance of the capital from limited partners.

Similar factors would be present in the Army equity fund. The private fund general partners are responsible for analyzing and assessing business opportunities, and they define the life of the fund through its investment and sale decisions. In return, the general partners receive organization expenses and placement fees of 2 to 3 percent, management fees that are typically about 2 percent per year, and 20 percent or more of total gains after return of capital. In the Army equity fund, the Army is a limited partner and is not involved with operating or investment decisions. The Army's return may be less than that of a general partner.

A primary benefit of an Army equity fund is that the Army can leverage its research funds using a highly focused investment strategy. The Army is isolated from direct investment decisions in individual companies, and conflict-of-interest issues can be minimized by government sale of interest if the public market is established or before production contracts are awarded. This scheme is applicable to most industry niches and can enhance innovation and competition in the defense second-tier industry market. This concept can also be attractive to firms with unique capabilities that are unwilling to compete for defense contacts.

An Army equity fund is likely to be legal, but like the OTJV, it may face some acceptance and attractiveness problems because of its novelty.

Leasing Technology with Option to Buy

Leasing technology with the option to buy is likely to be legal and publicly and politically acceptable as well as attractive to private firms. However, the Army owns much of the technology it uses, so the idea of leasing it may not be preferred. Leasing technology can help decrease Army outlays for technology.

Research Fund

The Army Research Office (ARO) has floated the idea of collecting R&D contributions from private firms and combining the money in a large research fund.[1] ARO would then distribute the money to fund research in dual-use technologies. The idea is that a combined fund will allow for funding dual-use research efforts that are beyond the reach of any one firm or the Army alone. ARO would choose the researchers from the academic community. One potential benefit to the Army is likely to be the ability to influence the technologies early

---

[1] Gerald Iafrate, ARO, private communication, 1997.

in their R&D phases. For some technologies, this type of PPP might be a good way for the Army to leverage some of its R&D funds. This idea is likely to be legal through 10 USC §2371, the Other Transactions legislation. Such a research fund is likely to be acceptable, but it might face some concerns from industry. The advantages to the firms contributing funds would have to be made clear and assured for industry to contribute.

Incubator Arrangement

An incubator arrangement is a venture in which the Army contributes a facility such as a research center and, perhaps, some infrastructure-support services such as secretarial assistance. Startup firms doing R&D in dual-use areas may use the facility and services, and in return the Army receives equity in the companies. This idea is likely to be legal, likely to be acceptable, and can be extremely attractive to startup firms with good ideas but not much cash. This idea has some precedent. The Army's Soldier Systems Command has proposed an idea similar to the incubator arrangement, and the University of Southern California has established the Egg Company 2 (EC^2) project in its Cinema School.[2] The Army could benefit from such an arrangement because it may afford ample opportunities for the Army to influence technologies early in their R&D phases. This type of PPP could also be a lucrative method of leveraging assets because if the startup company is successful, the Army will own equity in the firm that it can convert into discounted Army purchases or money to fund additional research.

FINANCIAL ARRANGEMENTS

Negotiate Discounts

For some purchases, it may be possible and appropriate for the Army to negotiate discounts. For example, the Naval Base Norfolk has created an energy vision plan to efficiently meet its energy demand over the next 25 years. One aspect of this plan is to use an agent to aggressively negotiate discounted prices with energy suppliers. The

---

[2] See Appendix B for more information about the Egg Company 2 (EC^2) project.

plan also calls for combining Naval Base Norfolk's energy needs with those of other DoD units in the area to maximize the negotiation posture and take full advantage of economies of scale and billing consolidation. The plan calls for the broker's profit to increase as the price to the Navy decreases. This type of arrangement is likely to be acceptable and could be attractive especially in situations where competition is present. This concept might be legal, but the Federal Acquisition Regulation (FAR) could be a barrier to its implementation. Discounts would benefit the Army in reducing its costs and outlays.

Negotiate Exchange Privileges

Exchange privileges may be appropriate for some of the equipment that the Army purchases. This practice may allow for expedient replacement of defective or ineffective equipment at lower cost. For example, partial credit might be negotiated for upgrading, or perhaps upgrades from the same firm could be had for a lower price in exchange for the older but still functional equipment. Clearly, there may only be a limited number of circumstances when this concept could apply. One situation might be where the Army's requirements change unexpectedly, and the equipment the Army exchanges is still being sold by the firm.

This concept is likely to be legal and acceptable and could also be attractive to firms. This idea can reduce costs and decrease outlays for needed equipment.

Nontraditional Cost Sharing

The Army has traditionally used money, personnel, and physical assets such as facilities as means for in-kind cost sharing. In some cases, other items may be appropriate. Options might include equity, future discounting, percentage of sales, free merchandise, complimentary services, credit, and shares in intellectual property ownership. At least some of these options might be legal, acceptable, and attractive; but the Army should expect obstacles to their use for in-kind cost sharing. Such an application, while novel, may also be difficult to implement. The benefits to the Army from using these options will vary depending on the exact terms of the PPP.

Auctions

There are many instances when the Army disposes of unneeded equipment by giving it away. An alternate means of disposing of unneeded equipment might be to auction it. This means is likely to be legal, acceptable, and attractive. It might also generate a small amount of revenue for the Army.

Army Affinity Credit Card

An affinity credit card is a credit card that provides usage rewards for cardholders and card sponsors. The rewards can take the form of frequent flyer miles, discounts on purchases, accumulation of bonus dollars, or funding for specific groups. The rewards can be split between the cardholder and the affinity group named on the card. In the case of an Army affinity credit card, the Army and the cardholder would split the rewards. Such a program would be similar to the Smithsonian affinity credit card, where the Smithsonian Institute receives a percentage of the purchase amount and the cardholder receives a $50 U.S. savings bond for every $5,000 of purchases. In the Army's case, it could consider other rewards to make the card more attractive to potential cardholders. For example, rewards could be contributions to medical savings accounts or other savings plans or to stock or mutual fund purchase plans.

In general, affinity cards pay royalty fees to the affinity group. The payments are usually equivalent to 0.5 percent of monthly purchases and balance transfers. If we assume an average usage of $300 of charges per month per cardholder, then the return per cardholder would be $18 per year. Assuming that the Army can attract 500,000 cardholders, the Army can realize $9M per year from an Army affinity card.

Affinity credit cards are probably legal and attractive mechanisms that can generate revenue for the Army.[3] The public might find the idea acceptable, but obstacles may arise in the political arena and within the Army.

---

[3]Recent discussions within the IRS may permit affinity card "donations" to be deducted. Such a deduction would make all affinity cards more attractive to the public.

Purchasing Rights

Purchasing rights is a provision placed into an agreement between the Army and a commercial firm from which the Army is planning to buy products. Such rights can be structured in many ways and can be used to accomplish a variety of purposes. For example, the Army may wish to provide a priori purchasing agreements with a vendor as an incentive to build a product needed by the Army. Another use is for the Army to use purchasing rights to allow it to buy certain products at predetermined prices before the products are released for public sale. This concept might be legal, acceptable, and attractive. It might also provide savings to the Army in select cases.

Project Finance

Project financing is a very specialized debt arrangement. A loan is arranged to finance a specific project. The security for the loan is the project itself. For example, the Army could try to secure a commercial loan to clean up a piece of "BRAC" land so that the land can be used for commercial development. In such a case, the piece of land would serve as security for the commercial loan. The loan would be paid back when the Army arranged for sale or commercial development of the environmentally safe piece of land. This type of project financing might not be legal and could face obstacles in acceptance. However, it might be attractive to commercial banks that wish to make such loans. This concept could allow the Army to undertake projects that will eventually bring a monetary return without investing any of its own funds.

Army Information Broker Service

The Army owns data bases and patents, some of which may have commercial value. Under an Army information broker service, Army-owned patents, test data, human test data, psychological profile data, and other such items are made available to commercial users for a fee. The fee might be an outright sale of a data base, or a per-use fee for specific data, or a percentage of returns for use of a patent. This concept could be implemented within the Army or could be contracted out to an outside partner. This idea could be viewed as an extension of the services now provided to NASA by the

Regional Technology Transfer Centers (RTTC).[4] RTTCs now attempt to facilitate the commercial use of defense technologies. Under the Army information broker services idea, not only would defense technologies be considered, but other Army products such as data bases would also be marketed. This idea could be attractive and possibly be a legal way to generate some revenue.

Army Loan Program

The Army could create a small-loans program for its members. The main purpose of such a program would be to provide a loan option for Army members. Such a program could be set up in a variety of ways and incorporate a number of provisions. One possible arrangement would be for the Army to enter into an agreement with a commercial lending institution. The institution would provide the funds for the loans and the Army would provide the customers. The Army could also guarantee the loans or serve as cosigner or automatically deduct loan payments from paychecks. In exchange, the commercial bank would pay the Army a predetermined fee that could be based on the amount of loans it actually makes, or the number of customers the Army provides, or some other metric. In this way, the Army can provide a useful service to its members and generate a small amount of revenue. An extension of this concept would be for the Army itself to act as the bank and make loans not only to its members, but to small businesses and the public as well. This extension might provide greater returns, but it would require the Army to adopt a function not related to its primary military mission. The legality of this idea is doubtful, although some lending institutions may find the concept attractive.

Army Real Estate Investment Trust

The Army real estate investment trust (REIT) idea combines a number of notions and can be set up in a variety of ways. One possible

---

[4]As this report goes to press the DoD is considering either joining the NASA RTTC program or starting an equivalent program of its own with a possible service lead. If the DoD proceeds along either of these paths, the Army will automatically be a part of an activity that has adopted the Information Fund concept. If the DoD does not proceed, then the Army should consider an Information Fund of its own.

implementation would be to view all the land and facilities that the Army leases out as a package, called a real estate trust. The trust can then be used to raise money from the financial markets. The commercial equivalent of this idea would be real estate investment trusts that are made up of shopping centers located in different areas but owned by a single owner. Such a trust is traded as a security on a stock exchange and could generate income to shareholders. In the Army REIT, the funds can be earmarked for a specific Army use. The legality and acceptance of this idea is doubtful, but it could be attractive to select private parties.

Appendix B
LIST OF EXAMPLES

This appendix contains an alphabetical listing of some current or proposed PPPs. Some of these programs have been used in the report to illustrate points, concepts, and approaches. For those examples that are used in the report, the chapter or section where the example is discussed is shown in parentheses following the summary paragraph. Some may not be related or applicable to the Army but are included for illustration purposes.

ADOPT-A-HIGHWAY PROGRAM

The Adopt-a-Highway program gives citizens' groups and businesses an opportunity to volunteer their time and energy to keep roadways clean and beautiful. Civic groups, schools, or private organizations can adopt a two-mile section of road by signing an agreement with the state transportation department and promising to pick up litter two or more times per year (varies by state). In return, the group is recognized for its service through road signs along the stretch of road it maintains and, in some cases, through other media. The program is an effective way to reduce a state's cost of litter pickup, which minimizes maintenance costs. Military bases could possibly initiate a similar program and adapt it for use throughout an installation and include areas other than just roadways. (Appendix A, "Financial Arrangements" subsection.)

Source: "Pennsylvania Adopt a Highway Program," Fact Sheet and Application Form, Copyright 1995 by Net Letters and VNCO; World Wide Web homepage: www.letters.com/vnco/highway.html.

ADVANCED SIMULATION PROJECTS

Army Research Lab (ARL) and the Communication-Electronics Command (CECOM) entered a CRADA with Silicon Graphics, Inc. (SGI) in an attempt to "improve simulation capabilities for dismounted soldiers, and the rest of the combined arms force." SGI has the simulation expertise and the computer technology needed by the Army to effectively process and analyze information. The agreement called for an exchange of technology and the protection of all intellectual property, but no monetary exchange. The Army will reap some of the benefits of SGI's investment in R&D, and SGI will gain insights into the Army's needs. SGI can use these insights in its product planning. (Chapter Two.)

Source: "Army Set to Ink Research Agreement with Silicon Valley Computing Giant," *Inside the Army,* Vol. 8, No. 42, October 21, 1996, pp. 1 and 13–15.

ARMAMENT RETOOLING AND MANUFACTURING SUPPORT (ARMS) PROGRAM

This program was initiated to avoid closing Army ammunition plants. Private firms use the plants for commercial purposes during peacetime, while maintaining and improving the facilities. In times of national emergency, the plants revert to Army control. Rental proceeds pay for maintenance and modernization and environmental remediation. (Chapter One.)

Source: "Conversion of Ammunition Plants Offer Once-in-a-Lifetime Opportunity," Operation Enterprise, News@ARMS, Issue 1.0, 1996.

ARMY FEDERATED LABORATORY

Federated Laboratory is the new Army Research Laboratory concept. This Army program with the private sector is an effort to leverage expertise in the areas of microelectronics and digital communications. Five-year Cooperative Agreements were executed in 1996 between the Army and three consortia. The consortia consist of members from industry and educational institutions and are required to spend upwards of 20 percent of their time working in each other's facilities. This close association benefits all parties. The consortia were formed for Advanced Sensors, Telecommunications/Information Distribution, and Advanced and Interactive Displays.

Source: *Army Research Laboratory Annual Review,* 1996, pp. 51–52; also, "Introduction, Federated Laboratory," World Wide Web homepage: http://www.arl.army.mil.

AUTOCAD ADD-ON PROGRAM

Engineers working for Naval Facilities Engineering Services at Port Hueneme designed an add-on program for AutoCad. The program allows AutoCad to be used in the design port facilities and "acts as a method of compiling and sharing installation related data." In order to facilitate the commercialization opportunities of the new program, the Navy entered into a CRADA with CadPLUS Products Company. The CRADA "authorizes CadPLUS to make necessary enhancements to existing Navy software to commercialize it, . . . it provides for continuous technological improvements, . . . and provides a limited number of copies, . . . for distribution to government agencies." The Navy also receives royalties on the sales of the technology.

Source: Al Antelman and Alex Miller, "A CAD Solution for Facility Management," *The Military Engineer,* Vol. 86, No. 565, August–September 1994.

CIVIL RESERVE AIRCRAFT FLEET PROGRAM

This program is a longstanding agreement between the military and major civilian airline companies. The government pays a fee to the airlines for the privilege of using their services and equipment to transport military personnel in times of emergency. (Chapter Three.)

Source: "Civil Reserve Air Fleet Fact Sheet," Office of Public Affairs, Scott AFB, Illinois; World Wide Web homepage: http://www.safb.af.mil/hqamc/pa/facts/craffact.htm.

EGG COMPANY 2 (EC²)

EC² is a multimedia incubator for new technologies with educational potential. It incubates new companies, new technologies, new ideas, and new relationships in the growing industries of interactive communiations. It brings together companies, entrepreneurs, academics, developers, and storytellers to provide insight and action to advance technology and content development. The program provides a controlled environment, housing approximately six software startups per year. The program is directed by the University of Southern California (USC) and funded by the Annenberg Foundation. In return, USC receives stock warrants in the startup firms that participate in the program. (Appendix A, "Intellectual Property" subsection.)

Source: EC² brochure, The Annenberg Center for Communication, University of Southern California; World Wide Web homepage: http://www.ec2.edu.

EASTERN HARBOR CROSSING DEVELOPMENT

The Eastern Harbor Crossing Development was a project that built a rail and motor tunnel connecting Quarry Bay on Hong Kong Island to Cha Kwo Ling, Kowloon, on the mainland of the People's Republic of China. This project received no public funds. The project was financed by integrating equity contributions with a debt package that consisted of revolving loans and installment sale facilities.

Source: "Public-Private Partnerships in Infrastructure: A Primer," Price Waterhouse Transportation and Utilities Finance Group, Washington, D.C., not dated, pp. 12–13.

HAND-HELD MULTI-MEDIA TERMINALS (HHMMTs)

The Army has formed a PPP involving an OT between Communications-Electronics Command (CECOM) and ITT. ITT will develop HHMMTs that will have both military and commercial usages. The Army receives the benefit of reduced cost and order priority when necessary. ITT benefits by being able to develop a commercial product with partial funding by the government. (Chapter One.)

Source: From Communications-Electronics Command, Fort Monmouth, NJ, "Agreement Completed Pursuant to 10 U.S.C. 2311 'Other Transactions' (DARPA)," DISUM, June 24, 1996.

HOT WEATHER AUTO TEST TRACK

The Army has approval to form a partnership with a vehicle manufacturer to build a test track at Yuma Proving Ground. The Army would provide a long-term land lease to an automobile manufacturer. The private firm would fund the construction and maintenance of the track. (Chapter Two.)

Source: *The Outpost*, U.S. Army Yuma Proving Ground Post Newspaper, Vol. 34, No. 31, October 27, 1997.

LONG BEACH NAVAL STATION LAND LEASE

The Navy is leasing 16 acres of underutilized land at Long Beach Naval Station to the Long Beach Port Authority. The lease is presently worth $50,000 per acre, with a total value of $800,000 per year. In lieu of the 1997 scheduled closure of the base, an increase in the amount of leased property could have generated increased funds for base use, while protecting the property for future use in case of national emergency. (Chapter One.)

Source: *California Military Bases Closures and Realignments: Current Status of Reuse Efforts (Long Beach Shipyard)*, report prepared by the Governor's Office of Planning and Research, State of California, not dated; World Wide Web homepage: http://www.cedar.ca.gov/military/current_reuse/longship.htm.

MAZDA SOUTHERN CALIFORNIA DISTRIBUTION CENTER

The Navy leases underutilized land at Port Hueneme to the Mazda Corporation. Mazda uses a fenced portion of the base as its Southern California Distribution Center, giving Mazda a convenient location. The Navy receives approximately $1.2 million per year in infrastructure improvements under the terms of the lease. (Chapter Three.)

Source: Private communication with Contracting Officer, Port Hueneme Navy CBC, on Mazda Lease, Contract Number N62474-96-RPOQ04, 1997.

NAVAL BASE NORFOLK ENERGY VISION

In 1996, the Norfolk Navy Base developed an energy vision in an effort to reduce energy cost while continuing to operate at optimum level and improve quality of life. A key element of the plan was to outsource energy procurement, which is not a Navy core strategic activity, to an agent who would manage this activity and aggressively negotiate with energy producers for the best prices and services. (Appendix A, "Financial Arrangements" subsection.)

Source: Naval Base Norfolk Energy Vision Statement, Department of the Navy, February 15, 1996.

NORFOLK PORT FACILITIES

The Navy has entered discussions with the Port Authority of Norfolk, Virginia for joint endeavors on Naval Base Norfolk. As with the Long Beach port facilities, the Navy could lease the facilities to the Norfolk Port Authority and retain usage rights in case of a national emergency. (Chapter Three.)

Source: Katherine McIntire Peters, "Funding the Fleet," *Government Executive,* January 1997, pp. 42–45.

RADAR IMAGING TECHNOLOGY

DARPA has an agreement signed in 1997 with Environmental Research Institute of Michigan (ERIM) that grants DARPA radar-imaging technology to ERIM. ERIM will commercialize the technology for use by both government and nongovernment entities. ERIM will pay royalties to DARPA out of the profits derived from commercial sales of resulting products. (Chapter Two.)

Source: Sandra Meadows, "Pentagon Bullish on Privately-Marketed Defense Technology," *National Defense,* April 1997, p. 16; "Agreement to Commercialize Government Funded Technology," DoD

News Release and Briefing, Office of the Assistant Secretary of Defense (Public Affairs), Ref. No. 063-97, February 11, 1997.

REGIONAL TECHNOLOGY TRANSFER CENTERS (RTTC) SYSTEM

Initiated by NASA in 1991, RTTCs have professional staff who contact companies and federal laboratories to help domestic companies locate, access, acquire and use technologies and expertise from NASA, federal labs, state agencies, and industry. The RTTCs expedite technology transfer and spur economic development by leveraging expertise of federal agencies to the civilian sector. For example, in 1994, the Northeast RTTC was instrumental in effecting a patent transfer between the Army Night Vision Directorate (CECOM) and S.E. International. The transfer allowed S.E. International to manufacture a dosimeter charger required by the Federal Emergency Management Agency. (Chapter Five.)

Source: *The RTTC System, RTTC System Notebook and Briefing Guide*, NASA, not dated; NASA Regional Technology Transfer Centers (RTTCs), Southern California Applications Center (STAC); World Wide Web homepage: http://www.state.ti.us/stac/centers.html.

SMITHSONIAN CARD

The Smithsonian Institution has a credit card agreement with the Novus Bank System. Novus supplies a credit card, the Smithsonian Card, to individuals wanting to contribute to the Smithsonian Institution in a unique way. By supplying the card, Novus receives the fees paid by vendors accepting the card, as well as interest paid by card users. The individual receives benefits such as competitive interest rates and points toward savings bonds. The Smithsonian Institution receives a percentage of every purchase made using the card, plus a contribution for every card issued or renewed. (Chapter Four.)

Source: "The Smithsonian Card—Information Center," Novus Bank Corp., not dated; World Wide Web homepage: www.novusnet.com/smithsonian/data/info.htm.

SOLDIER HOUSING

Two thousand Fort Drum housing units, and the land they occupy, are owned and operated by four companies in the area of Watertown, New York. The developers purchased the land and built the housing at the request of the Army. Fort Drum in turn leases the units for occupancy by soldiers assigned to the installation. The developers are responsible for all maintenance and upkeep of the facilities. This operation saves the Army from the responsibility of maintenance and also provides readily available housing to the soldiers. (Chapter Four.)

Source: Steve M. Friedman, Wallace A. Little, and Paul A. Penler, "Solving the Military Housing Dilemma," reprint from *EYKL's Real Estate Online Magazine*, The E&Y Kenneth Levanthal Real Estate Group, Number One, 1997.

SPIDER SILK STUDY

The Army collaborates with the Center for Biotechnology at Cornell University and other commercial firms to jointly research the properties and uses of spider silk. Spider silk is lightweight yet strong and could be used in fabric that would lighten a soldier's load. The Army will receive 1 percent royalties from any patent resulting from the program. Resulting products could also have commercial application. Under the agreement, the Army will receive order priority in the event quick acquisition is necessary. (Chapter One.)

Source: Private communication with Natick Research, Development, and Engineering Center, U.S. Soldiers Systems Command, 1997.

THAYER HOTEL, WEST POINT

A leasing action should be finalized in the November-December 1997 time frame. Under the agreement, Hudson River Partners (HRP) will take over the Thayer Hotel from the Army, under the terms of a 50-year lease. HRP will renovate the hotel, operate it during the lease term, add a state-of-the-art conference facility, and collect all sales receipts. All costs will be incurred by HRP. The Army will benefit by the availability of a totally renovated and improved facility on the installation, the receipt of 1 percent of gross sales each quarter, and resumption of control of an improved facility at the end of the lease. (Chapter Two.)

Source: *Thayer Hotel Privatization: Public Affairs Guidance,* U.S. Army Community and Family Support Center, approved by Peter F. Isaacs, Deputy Commander (Programs), U.S. Army Community and Family Support Center, not dated.

VERY HIGH-SPEED BACKBONE NETWORK SERVICE

In 1995, the National Science Foundation (NSF) awarded a five year cooperative agreement to MCI to build the vBNS. The vBNS allows NSF to "transmit massive amounts of voice, data, and video at speeds nearly four times faster than current technology." The NSF uses the technology to link teams of scientists at five supercomputer centers who work at such tasks as trying to predict global climate changes.

Source: *MCI and the Internet Backbone,* MCI Telecommunications Corp., Copyright 1997; World Wide Web homepage: http://www.mci.com/mcisearch/aboutyou/interests/technology/internet/iback.shtml.

WILLOUGHBY HOUSING DEVELOPMENT

The Navy is interested in developing a narrow slice of waterfront at the Norfolk Naval Station called the Willoughby Housing Development. According to this plan, a developer would raze the dilapidated apartments and replace them with a hotel-office-marina complex and upscale townhouses. The Navy would use the proceeds from the leased property to provide housing elsewhere for Navy personnel. (Chapter Five.)

Source: Katherine McIntire Peters, "Funding the Fleet," *Government Executive,* January 1997, pp. 42–45.

YUMA PROVING GROUND HOTEL

A private firm will develop a hotel on Army property. The commercial firm will fund the building project and then operate the hotel when it is completed. The commercial firm gains profits, while the Army benefits by receiving a percentage of the profits and retaining ownership of the land. (Chapter One.)

Source: *The Outpost*, U.S. Army Yuma Proving Ground Post Newspaper, Vol. 34, No. 31, October 17, 1997, pp. 1, 3.

BIBLIOGRAPHY

Alexander, Gordon, William Sharpe, and Jeffrey Bailey, *Fundamentals of Investment,* Englewood Cliffs, NJ: Prentice Hall, 1993

Antelman, Al, and Alex C. Miller, "A CAD Solution for Facility Management," *The Military Engineer,* August–September 1994, Volume 86, Number 565.

Army Teams with Industry, *Inside the Army,* Vol. 8, No. 42, October 21, 1996.

"Conversion of Ammunition Plants Offer Once-in-a-Lifetime Opportunity," *Operation Enterprise,* News@ARMS, Issue 1.0, 1996.

DARPA Acquisition Conference, "Use of the 10 USC 2371 and Section 845 Authorities," March 17–18, 1997.

Dunn, Richard L., "DARPA Turns to 'Other Transactions,'" *Aerospace America,* October 1996, pp. 33–37.

Dunn, Richard L., "Other Applications for 'Other Transactions,'" *Aerospace America,* September 1997.

Feldman, Roger D., "Privatization: What Is It, How Does It Work?" Special Federal Privatization Issue, *Translational Finance,* McDermott, Will & Emery, March 1995, Vol. 7, No. 1, pp. 1–6.

Federal Technology Transfer Act of 1986, Public Law 99-502.

Federated Laboratory (Fed Lab), ARL, Federated Laboratory Web Homepage, http://w3.arl.mil/mgtinit/mgtflab.html.

Horn, Kenneth, et al., "Generating Revenue to Help Offset Declining Infrastructure and R&D Budgets," unpublished RAND research, 1997.

Horn, Kenneth, Elliot Axelband, Ike Chang, Paul Steinberg, Carolyn Wong, Howell Yee, *Performing Collaborative Research with Nontraditional Military Suppliers,* Santa Monica, CA: RAND, MR-830-A, 1997.

"Inside the Pentagon—Special Report," February 6, 1997.

Keogh, Patrick J., and Kim McCarson, "Procurement: The Enemy Within," *Government Executive,* August 1997, pp. 69–70.

Kuyath, Richard N., "The Untapped Potential of the Department of Defense's 'Other Transactions' Authority," *Public Contract Law Journal,* Vol. 24, No. 4, September 1995, pp. 521–577.

Meadows, James E., "Lowry: A Role Model for Base Redevelopment," *Urban Land,* March 1997, pp. 26–29 and 64–65.

"Military Housing Assistance Act," Memorandum from Commander in Chief, U.S. Atlantic Fleet, to Secretary of the Navy, October 26, 1996.

Morella, Chairwoman Constance A., Introductory Statement of H.R. 2544, Technology Subcommittee, September 30, 1997.

NASA Regional Technology Transfer Centers (RTTCs), Southern Technology Applications Center (STAC) World Wide Web pages, http://www.state.ti.us/stac/centers.html.

National Technology Transfer and Advancement Act of 1995, Public Law 104-113.

Naval Base Norfolk Energy Vision Statement, Department of the Navy, February 15, 1996.

Office of the Assistant Secretary of Defense (Public Affairs), News Release, "DoD, ERIM and Intermap Technologies Sign Innovative Agreement," Ref. No. 063-97, February 11, 1997.

Peters, Katherine McIntire, "Funding the Fleet," *Government Executive,* January 1997, pp. 42–45.

Public-Private Partnerships in Infrastructure: A Primer, Washington, D.C., Price Waterhouse, Transportation and Utilities Finance Group, Washington, D.C.

RDT&E Programs (R-1) Department of Defense Budget for Fiscal Year 1997, March 1996.

Report of the Defense Science Board 1996 Summer Study on Achieving an Innovative Support Structure for 21st Century Military Superiority: Higher Performance at Lower Costs, Defense Science Board, Washington, DC, November 1996.

Report of the Defense Science Board Task Force on Defense Acquisition Reform (Phase III): A Streamlined Approach to Weapons Systems Research, Development and Acquisition: The Application of Commercial Practices, Defense Science Board, Washington, DC, May 1996.

Report of the National Defense Panel, Transforming Defense— National Security in the 21st Century, December 1997.

Report of the Quadrennial Defense Review, William S. Cohen, Secretary of Defense, Department of Defense, May 1997.

Report to Congress, "Vision 21: The Plan for 21st Century Laboratories and Test and Evaluation Centers of the Department of Defense," April 30, 1996.

The RTTC System, RTTC System Notebook and Briefing Guide, NASA.

Sources of Funds for Army Use (Other Than Typical Army Appropriations), Office of the Assistant Secretary of the Army for Financial Management, Resource Analysis and Business Practices, SAFM-RB, July 1995.

Stainback, John, "Advantages of Public/Private Development Partnerships," *Urban Land,* July 1997, pp. 24–27 and 60–64.

Technology Transfer Commercialization Act of 1997 (Proposed), H.R. 2544.

United States Code, Title 10, Chapter 139, Section 2358, "Research and Development Projects."

United States Code, Title 10, Chapter 139, Section 2371, "Advanced Research Projects: Transactions Other Than Contracts and Grants."

United States Code, Title 10, Chapter 159, Section 2667, "Leases: Non-Excess Property."

United States Code, Title 10, Chapter 159, Section 2671, "Military Reservations and Facilities: Hunting, Fishing, and Trapping."

United States Code, Title 10, Chapter 159, Section 2681, "Use of Test and Evaluation Installations by Commercial Entities."

United States Code, Title 15, Chapter 63, Sections 3701–3714, "Technology Innovation."

United States General Accounting Office, *Defense Acquisition Infrastructure: Changes in RDT&E Laboratories and Centers*, GAO/NSIAD-96-221BR, September 1996.

Virginia Intermodal Partnership Project Report, June 1996.

Walker, Wayne G., *Technological Innovation, Corporation R&D Alliances and Organizational Learning*, Santa Monica, CA: RAND, RGSD-118, 1995.

Wong, C., *An Analysis of Collaborative Research Opportunities in the Army*, Santa Monica, CA: RAND, MR-675-A, 1998.

DATE DUE

DEMCO 38-297